RECREATING

PATRICK

An Inside Job

Patrick Harrington
with Kristine Meier-Skiff

GIFT AN AUTHOR PUBLISHING, LLC

Gift an Author Publishing, LLC
5405 Zara Drive
Denton, Texas, 76207
www.giftanauthor.com

ISBN: 9798990035508 (Paperback)
Library of Congress Control Number: 00000000000

Any references to historical events, real people, or places are fictitious. Names, characters, and places are products of the author's imagination.

Contents

INTRODUCTION

"Each meeting occurs at the precise moment for which it was meant. Usually, when it will have the greatest impact on our lives."

- Nadia Scrieva, Fathoms of Forgiveness

K ristine:

Come sit down, have a cup of coffee, and listen as I tell you about a man that changed my life. Our relationship started as a business connection but has developed into a meaningful friendship over the three years we worked together.

Patrick Harrington puts his entire self into whatever he does. I remember listening, entranced, as Patrick told me a summary of his life, the story he wanted me to write. It was like listening to the script for a movie, only this was real life. He was (and is) larger than life; his story enthralled me as a listener and even more so as a writer. This is the kind of story that every writer longs to write.

It was clear that the roads Patrick Harrington took to arrive on July 14, 1986, were long and winding, full of detours, wrong turns, and close calls. Maybe at one time, he thought the road would go on forever and the party would never end. Still, the warning signs, exit signs, and flashing cherry tops in his rear-view mirror suggested otherwise.

Seeing him today, you would be hard-pressed to imagine the trouble he's seen, much less the trouble he's caused. He's tall, solid, and still lives a relatively active life despite the hard years he and his body have been through. If his body had an odometer, it would have already turned over a couple of times. However, he's not only still standing, he's still moving and seeking out the next big adventure of his time.

Now you will probably find Patrick at his home in Cody, Wyoming. Here he and his wife, Olivia, have carved out a peaceful life surrounded by the mountains' beauty and the animals they love. When Patrick is not at home, he can be found at rodeos and trade shows selling his uniquely designed and quality southwestern-style rugs. He is hard to miss, an impressive man, towering over everyone in his cowboy boots, a handcrafted cowboy belt, and cowboy hat.

Over the past 35 years, he has built a successful company, SkyHawk rugs. He is a respected businessman, having brokered million-dollar deals around the world. But even in his success, he does not forget where he came from. He uses his company's success to support veterans and recovering addicts. Patrick is a man who remembers where he came from and is determined to help all those that he can on their journeys. This is one of the qualities that I most admire about him.

All the roads of Patrick's life converged in 1986 when he took his last drink and his last hit of cocaine. If he had known what it would take to turn himself into someone sober and that lived everyday life with integrity and honor, he would never have started down that road. It has been a long and challenging process that has brought him to his knees and tested the limits of his sanity more times than he can count. He could never have imagined the adventurous and wonderful life he would enjoy as a major drug dealer and trafficker in the depths of his addiction.

Patrick is very spiritual. This spirituality has held him steady through the hard times and the good times. But his faith is practical and down-to-earth. Having seen God's grace and protection in his life, he knows God loves everyone.

He doesn't judge anyone as he has lived through his own mistakes and fought his own demons. Instead of quoting scriptures to people, he shows his faith through how he lives his life, in humility, with honesty, and by practicing charity. He is a silent knight in a world of screaming knaves.

In his words, "*Religion is for people who don't want to go to hell. Spirituality is for those who have already been there.*" He would know as he has been to hell and back.

However, to understand where Patrick ended up, we must go back nearly sixty years to an orphanage in Fort Wayne, Indiana. This is where the forge fires that created the man that is Patrick Harrington were laid, lit, and stoked.

The Prayer of Jabez

And Jabez called on the God of Israel, saying, 'Oh that You would bless me indeed, and enlarge my territory. That Your hand would be with me, and that You would keep me from evil, that I may not cause pain!' So God granted him what he requested.
1 Chronicles 4:10

CHAPTER ONE

The Tricycle

"Any strengths I may have come out of much loss and sadness."

- Patrick Harrington

My first memories are of my time spent in the orphanage: the sounds of my baby sister Lora's cries that echoed as she cried herself to sleep far away from where I could comfort her, the mush of inedible oatmeal, the sting of the nun's hand as she slapped me across the face, the feel of my tooth tearing through the flesh of my lip. These memories, my origin story, have haunted me for a lifetime. They are the painful foundations on which I built my life.

I was born Patrick Harrington on a fall day in Indianapolis, Indiana, to Catholic Irish American parents.

My father, Thomas Harrington, was born in Dunkirk, Indiana, where his immigrant family had moved to work at the Indiana Glass Factory.

In 1886 natural gas was discovered in Howard County. It wasn't long before that discovery led to a boom in factory work bringing many immigrant families desperate to fill the jobs. My family was among them, looking to make a new life for their families away from the poverty and bigotry that plagued them on the east coast.

My father's aunt adopted him after his mother, Agnes, died due to childbirth complications a few months after delivering him. His mother was also adopted, though the why for that adoption is now unknown. Displaced children are a common thread throughout my family history.

My father was probably bipolar, a manic depressive. Dad wasn't a raging alcoholic. But, he was an Irishman who could put away the booze when the need arose. During World War II, he served in the U.S. Navy from 1943–45.

He came home chasing after several dreams until finally becoming a Tin Man. The movie *Tin Men* starring Richard Dreyfus, provides a pretty accurate picture of my father's life, a siding salesman willing to do anything—legal or not—to make a sale.

My mother, Rita Jarvis Harrington, was raised in Albany, Indiana. Her grandfather, Joshua Jarvis, was a retired minister and wallpaper hanger who died in 1918. While on his way home from a long work day, pulling a wallpaper cart, he was hit by a train while crossing the tracks. My great-grandmother, Laura Jarvis, was devastated. He had safely walked that route for years! What had happened on that day?

After an investigation, it was determined the railroad company was at fault. She sued them and was awarded ten thousand dollars as compensation. Ten thousand dollars in 1918 was a small fortune, worth just under two hundred thousand dollars in today's money.

Despite the large settlement, my mother did not have an easy childhood. She and her sisters were systematically sexually abused by their father. Her mother was ill, bedridden, and unable to protect them. She once told me that she would quietly creep into her mother's room every day after school, terrified she would find her dead in her bed. That constant fear of loss traumatized my mother, making her unable to form healthy attachments with other people.

School became her sanctuary from the horrors that awaited her at home. But even there, she was violated. One of her male teachers saw her vulnerability and raped her in her classroom. She was traumatized repeatedly throughout her childhood, but there was little understanding of PTSD and its lasting effects back then. Instead, she tried to face the world with no way to fight the demons that plagued her.

Those demons led to mental illness, addiction, and sexual promiscuity. She spent time in mental wards off and on throughout our growing-up years. Because of her childhood, my mother had no idea how to nurture us. Thus the cycle of trauma and abuse continued for my siblings and me.

My parents were very young when they married. My Dad was 22, and my mom was only 20. They quickly started our family, having my five siblings and me back to back, as was the way for most Catholic families in our generation. I was the second oldest child and the oldest boy in our family. That responsibility was always important to me. I did my best to provide for my family, even when our parents didn't.

Their marriage and our family life were tumultuous from the start. My father was a salesman who was a big dreamer with big plans but few ways to accomplish those dreams. Later in my life, he would become a small-time gangster, always looking for the next big score. He always knew a guy who knew a guy. He and his friends were small-time criminals trying to gain respect through association.

Though she and my father truly loved us and did their best, they had no idea how to raise kids while fighting severe poverty and struggling with mental health and addiction. Years later, as an adult, my psychologist commented on how I must resent them for how they failed us as parents. She was surprised when I told her that I had forgiven them and understood that they did their best with what they had. I'll never forget what she said: "*Well, they still did a shitty job.*" That about sums it up. My parents did their best, I loved them, but they still did a shit job of parenting.

Saint Vincent Orphanage

 When I was four years old, they again split up. My dad was struggling as a salesman. My mom started working at a curtain factory but was admitted to the mental hospital. Poverty was beating on our door, and my father could not afford to feed or care for us. With

few other options, we were dropped off at Saint Vincent Catholic Orphanage in Fort Wayne, Indiana. My sisters Mary, Lora, and I went to the orphanage. While our brother Michael, who was still an infant, was sent to live with our grandmother.

It was there that I have my earliest memories. I remember we didn't understand what would happen when he brought us there on that terrible day. We didn't understand that he was leaving us and wouldn't be coming back any time soon. Once the reality of our situation hit, we were inconsolable, crying, and our little hearts breaking. The nuns just went through the motions of getting us situated. I don't remember them comforting us at all.

I later learned that they called this "The Dump." Because parents dumped their kids off.

My younger sister Lora and I were placed in different rooms in one wing. While our older sister, Mary, who was too old to be in the same area, was put in the wing for older children. The memory of my sister Lora's cries reverberating off the walls still ring in my ears. I still remember the helplessness I felt because I couldn't comfort her. This developed a strong urge to protect and care for my siblings that has carried me throughout my life.

I was placed in a large sterile dorm-style room filled with kids, some true orphans and others in similar situations to ours. It was terrifying to be yanked away from everything I'd ever known and put in this cold and unfamiliar place. The nuns swarmed around the orphanage like a flock of overworked penguins, providing little warmth or comfort. I was scared and felt rejected, abandoned, and alone.

I remember another young boy about my age who slept on the cot beside mine. There was a donated teddy bear that we shared between us. If I was upset, he would give it to me, and I would give it to him when he was sad. Though I cannot remember his name, I often think of him to this day and wonder what became of him.

When the weather permitted, the nuns would bring us outside. I loved our moments in the fresh air, running around and playing. When it was time to go inside, they would choose a child to gather up the tricycles and put them away. Every day, I anxiously waited to be selected as the special kid on tricycle duty. In my young mind, tricycle duty made you needed and important. I desperately wanted to be needed. Every day, I waited to be the important tricycle kid. Every day I was disappointed as another kid was picked.

Looking back, I realize it wasn't personal. I was just too young to be left alone. But at the time, it felt like another rejection. Once again, I was not necessary or important. I would spend a good chunk of my life chasing after that feeling of importance. I wanted to, needed to, be the big man in charge, the one making big money and pulling the strings from the shadows. After all, when you are the head honcho, you matter. When you matter, you won't be abandoned or rejected.

I have other memories of my time in the orphanage. The dining room was a large room that felt cavernous and cold to me as a child. Three meals a day, we would line up with our plates or bowls to be served and sit at the long wooden tables lining the room. I clearly remember the smell, texture, and taste of the breakfast oatmeal we were fed daily. It was an inedible bowl of mush that tasted like wallpaper paste. I hated that oatmeal from the bottom of my four-year-old heart. My older sister Mary and I constantly looked for ways to get out of eating it. Mary would hide the cold mush in her socks and dump it on the playground.

I tried to get rid of it by sliding my bowl across the table to the boy across from me. I pushed the bowl too hard several times, and it slid past him, shattering on the hard floor. The second time I broke the bowl, the head nun decided to teach me a lesson. She picked me up and roughly placed me in a simple wooden highchair. She told me if I wanted to act like a baby, I would be treated like one. When I again refused to eat the horrible oatmeal, she repeatedly slapped me across the face so hard that my tooth tore through my bottom lip. I still remember the chill on my face from the ice one of the other nuns put on my lip to stop the bleeding and swelling.

It's the first time I remember coming out of my body. I just wanted to be somewhere else. I blocked out everything around me from my mind and floated away to somewhere safe. You can call it PTSD or whatever you want, but that's how it happened.

Years later, when I finally got my records from the orphanage, no mention was made of this incident. However, there is a small note documenting that a dentist was needed to address an unspecified injury. They definitely covered their asses in the notes. To this day, I cannot tolerate the look, smell, or taste of oatmeal. I would rather go hungry than eat that awful gruel.

Some of my memories of this time are just flashes of images with no real context. Often, they come to me when I least expect them. Once, I walked into my friend Keith's saddle shop and saw a bathtub he uses to soak leather. It is a child-sized, claw-footed, cast iron tub on an old pedestal mounted to the wall. Suddenly, I was back in the orphanage, remembering a similar bathtub mounted to a wall where the nuns would bathe us. I assume they mounted the bathtub so they wouldn't have to bend down while washing so many young children. I have no specific memory attached to this image, but seeing that tub in my friend's shop makes me uncomfortable. The mind is strange in what it does and doesn't remember. I may never know why that tub has such an emotional impact on me. But for some reason, four-year-old me really disliked it.

I recently remembered that our Dad would visit and take us out for a few hours. He had a tape recorder and would record us talking. I don't know what happened to those tapes, but I wish I could listen to them now. We loved seeing him. However, after a few hours, he would drop us back at the orphanage, and it was like being abandoned all over again. Every time he did that, we would be in tears, begging that he take us home. I know it must have torn him up inside having to leave us, but as kids, we didn't understand what was happening. All we knew was he was leaving us again.

Several years ago, I wrote and asked for my records from my time at the orphanage. When the envelope finally arrived, I was surprised by how anxious I felt about getting it. It took me a full two weeks to work up the nerve to open it!

The records didn't contain any new revelations. They just documented my age, height, weight, and brief notes from the nuns. They reported that I was agreeable and wanted to please them and the note about the dentist. However, among the pages of ordinary minutia were treasures, letters written by my parents. These letters, written in both my parents' hands, were full of anguish and grief at the loss of us. They reached across the years and the grave to bring healing to my heart and the hearts of my sisters.

When it was all said and done, our time at St. Vincent's Orphanage changed something fundamental within us. My parents then reunited and were on better footing financially, so we could go home again. But we would never again feel completely secure that we would always have a home with our parents.

Addendum

While writing this book, I developed a deep need to buy my own tricycle. I needed to take back a little bit of myself that life had stolen from me.

For months I looked on eBay, trying to find a vintage tricycle like the ones they had at St. Vincent's Orphanage. Finally, I found it! It was beat-up, rusted, and was showing its age (a little like me), but it was exactly like the tricycles from my four-year-old memory.

After a few minutes of internal debate, overcoming that old part of myself that tried to convince me that I didn't need this or deserve it, I placed the bid. As the days of the auction ticked by, I nervously checked on the trike. Occasionally, I upped my bid. Now that I had decided to have it, nothing and no one would get in the way.

In the final moments of the auction, I was on pins and needles, hoping no one would swoop in at the last moment and outbid me. The timer hit zero. I looked, and I had the winning bid! I was ecstatic. It felt like a hole I had carried in my heart since I was four years old had been filled.

The next day, I saw an email from the seller. I excitedly opened it expecting it to confirm the tricycle's shipping details. Instead, it informed me that the seller could no longer sell the trike to me. I was crushed! All the feelings of inadequacy, disappointment, and abandonment I had felt as a four-year-old boy rushed over me. The elusive tricycle was still beyond my reach. I spiraled into a depressive episode that lasted the rest of the day.

The next morning I awoke, looked at myself in the mirror, and realized I was no longer a powerless four-year-old. I was a successful business owner that had been to hell and back and lived to tell the tale. A tricycle was not going to bring me down. Come what may, that trike would be mine!

Being the owner of a business that often ships large items, I ventured to guess that the seller had not realized how expensive it would be to ship. I wrote another email asking if that was indeed the case and telling him why this trike was so important to me.

Within a few short minutes, my phone dinged. I received an answer to my email! Somewhat nervously, I opened and read the response. It was from the owner of the company, Jason. He admitted that they underestimated the shipping cost but still had the tricycle. I offered to use my shipping account to reduce costs, and he agreed to send it to me. He told me how touched they had been by my story and that he knew the tricycle was meant to be mine.

I mentioned that I was writing this book and would like to share this story with those reading my story. He happily agreed and asked to be mentioned. Thank you, Jason, for being a part of my journey.

I was overwhelmed by the emotions that washed over me once I received confirmation that it had shipped. At four, I had no control over anything that happened to me. But as a man in his seventies, I had earned everything I ever had through grit, determination, and sometimes sheer stubbornness. After over sixty years, I was going to put away the tricycle. I didn't need anyone else to choose me because I could now choose myself. And there was great healing in that.

CHAPTER TWO

To Be a Pin Setter

"If I was a drinking man, I would be drinking right now. The problem is... I don't drink."

- Patrick Harrington

I remember the years immediately after leaving the orphanage as good ones. Our family moved to Walnut Avenue in Muncie, Indiana, because my father got a good job working for a concrete block company. This gave us the financial stability that had always been lacking. We lived in a nice house that had a basement. At the end of our street was a statue of Chief Muncie, arms outstretched to the sky, as he sat astride his horse.

In Muncie, my youngest sisters, Bridgette and Angela, were born. My mom was more emotionally stable for those first years we were back together and was trying hard to be a good mom. One of my fondest memories is fingerpainting in the basement with her. I can still feel the cold squish of the paint as I smeared it across the smooth paper. Maybe this was the start of my love of all forms of art. Who knows?

Back then, cowboy shows were all the rage. Davy Crockett, The Lone Ranger, and Gun Smoke taught an entire generation what it was to be a man and a hero. They were tall, good-looking, wore a cowboy or coonskin hat, did the right thing, and always got the girl. However, they lived a life of solitude in the wilderness between heroic episodes. These men represented everything I longed for in my own life: strength, adventure, and someone who would always be there when I needed them. I always wore my cowboy hat and boots, but the cowboy belt was one thing I didn't have. I wanted to own a cowboy belt the way a bear craves honey.

For a time, Alice was our babysitter though I have no idea how they paid her as we were poorer than church mice. She was the person that taught me how to save money. She gave me an old tin can and told me to put any change I earned in there if I wanted to get my belt. I saved all the pennies, nickels, and dimes I could in that old can. Then one day, I finally had enough money to buy my very own cowboy belt!

I was so excited as Alice walked me downtown to buy it. She praised me because I earned and saved the money by myself. I was only five or six, but I still remember the pride I felt after buying that belt. From that point onward, I realized I didn't have to go without what I needed or wanted. I had the power to earn my own money and make my way. Financial stability and independence were revolutionary concepts for a child that had only known abject poverty.

Pin Boys

When I was around eight or nine, I loved hanging out behind the bowling alley and watching the pin boys. They always kept the back

door open propped open. I would watch them through the screen door, the smells of machine oil, cigarette smoke, and the lane polish mixing into a unique scent I can almost smell today. I eavesdropped while they joked around and swapped stories over the crashing sounds of the bowling

balls hitting pins, the whirring of old fans, and the gears of the semi-automatic pinsetter machines.

They were the behind-the-scenes guys, collecting the knocked-down pins and putting them into the pinsetter machine that would put them on the lanes. It was a fast-paced, sweaty, and hot job. Pin Boys were a rough group of guys, sweating in the sauna-like conditions behind the lanes. They were young guys streaked in machine grease, cigarettes hanging from their lips, with vocabularies that would make sailors blush. And I thought they were cool as hell.

I wanted to be a pin boy more than anything else. Though no one saw them, they were needed. Without them, there would be no bowling. Like the tricycle collectors, pin boys were important, and I wanted to be important. Important boys don't get abandoned in orphanages or ignored at home. They were obsolete when I was old enough to be a pin boy, replaced with fully automatic pin-setting machines. I was left to find another way to become important.

Racism

Muncee is also where I first encountered racism. My father was a good man in many ways; he was a veteran of World War II, a patriot, and an optimist who never stopped dreaming. Still, he was prejudiced like many of his generation. He had no problem using the slur *"nigger"* when referring to people of color.

One day, when I was around five, our babysitter, a wonderful and gracious black lady, took us to her house. I don't remember why; I would guess my mom had to work. However, I did not want to go and was not shy about that fact. I clearly remember calling her a *"nigger."* I remember the shame I felt as soon as the word left my mouth. Though I had heard it said by the adults around me my whole life, I instinctively knew that word was not a nice thing to say. Even as small children, we know right from wrong; we have consciences.

Indiana was an epicenter for race riots and discrimination through the 1960s. Unfortunately, this would not be my last experience with the ugliness of racism.

Grandma Smith's House

I always loved visiting my Grandma Smith's house. To this day, certain smells remind me of her. I thought she lived in Dunkirk, Indiana's largest and most luxurious house. At least, it looked that way to my young eyes. Later, when I returned to the house as an adult, I realized it was just an average house. But when you are a child,

everything is larger, whether it is your grandma's house or your feelings.

During one visit, she told me our priest was coming to visit. While waiting, I played with Mexican Jumping Beans. It was the first time I had ever played

with them. Being a curious, ordinary young boy, I wanted to know what made them jump. So I broke one open to figure it out. Imagine my surprise when I found the worm inside! How cool was that? I stopped playing with the beans and started playing with the squishy little worm. Rolling it around in my hands was so much fun until I accidentally killed it.

My young heart was devastated, ashamed, and afraid. I just knew the priest would tell me I was going to hell for killing that poor worm. This was the first time that I remember experiencing the feeling of guilt. I was so afraid of what the priest would say or do to me that I hid from him. Guilt and shame; these emotions came early and would haunt me for a long time. To escape them, I would continue to hide. But unlike the five-year-old me who hid in a closet, my hiding places of choice were at the bottom of a bottle or the end of a line of cocaine.

Though our time in Muncee was the most stable our family would ever be, the cracks of dysfunction were widening. My father was fired from the concrete block company. When I was older, I learned he was fired for embezzlement. Once again out of work, it was time to leave Muncee and follow my father's next big dream: starting a pizza shop.

Marion, Indiana

Marion, Indiana, was a gritty Midwestern factory town of about 40,000 people when I was young. It was a blue-collar, shot-and-a-beer kind of town. A place where people worked and played hard and did what they had to do to get by. In the 1960s, the city extended the holiday season throughout the year with Christmas tree lights in the park and alongside the Mississinewa River, earning it the nickname Christmas City, USA.

Our house in Marion was down the street from Matter Park. Established in 1890, it is the oldest and largest park in Marion. We would walk to it, play on the playground, or simply hang out there. Years later, I discovered that there were rides in the park that you could ride for .25 cents. I find it strange that I don't remember those rides. But that is just another example of poverty's effect on you. We had no money to ride the rides. So the rides didn't exist for us. Therefore, I don't remember them.

It was here that my father, Daddy Man'O Fats, as we called him, set up his pizza shop. It is also where he got sucked deeper into the small-time criminal world he was a part of. I was always close to my Dad. I would ride with him as he picked up cheese or bought other supplies. I was proud of his pizza shop. All the teenagers would come to hang out, order pizza, and play songs on the jukebox.

Though not much of a businessman, my Dad made the best pizza (I still believe that to this day). He was also creative in getting business. He was the first to start delivering pizzas to the factory workers who worked shift work. No one was doing that kind of thing back then.

His business did well until the IRS audited him for not paying taxes. Things got so bad that the IRS would show up at the shop and take money directly from the register. Stunts like that wouldn't fly today, but it was a different world back then. I think it was then that his shady friends became even more important to him. While the business struggled, he could still be a big man around them.

When I think about it, I realize that my Dad also wanted to be important, to matter. Many of the demons I fought are the same ones my parents wrestled with. I don't blame them for my choices; I forgave them for their bad decisions years ago. However, dysfunction breeds dysfunction, and the broken break others. I came from broken parents, who broke me, and I later broke others. Thank God that none of us have to stay broken; we can do the work and become whole again.

Amid the chaos, we still had good times with Dad. He was a large man who loved sweet things. He would send us to the bowling alley down the street to buy a case of Hershey's chocolate bars. He would then give us one candy bar and eat the rest himself. He would make fudge or pop popcorn, and then we would watch tv together. Our favorite shows were Tarzan, The Twilight Zone, and Western shows like The Lone Ranger.

My Dad was a complicated man. Despite all of the dysfunction, I learned a lot from him. I remember sitting with him on the sofa, watching President Kennedy's funeral. He had tears streaming down his face as little John-John Kennedy saluted his father's flag-draped casket. The grief of the entire nation was palpable during that time. People were crying and talking about the horror of what happened in Dallas everywhere you went. But it is the tears of my father that are seared into my memory. I learned a lot about true patriotism from him that day.

My parents started hanging out at a bar named The Green Duck. The Green Duck was known for their pork tenderloin sandwiches, a local delicacy. These sandwiches were something else; the pork was pounded thin, fried, and loaded onto a bun with all the fixings. They were humongous, about the size of a dinner plate!

When my parents were heading to the bar, we'd ask them to bring us home a tenderloin sandwich. Sometimes they brought home a couple of them, sometimes only one, but usually, they forgot because they were drunk off their asses.

Things at home began to deteriorate quickly. Though they both drank, my Dad wasn't an alcoholic and could handle his drink much better than my mom. With her drunkenness came mental instability, carousing, and fights. I would wake up terrified at three in the morning, listening to my parents yelling at each other and fighting. More than once, my father had to restrain my mother to keep her from hurting him or herself. Sometimes he crossed the line from protection to abuse.

The more unstable their relationship became, the more they disappeared from our lives, leaving us to fend for ourselves. Often there was no food in the house at all. I would find whatever money I could and walk down to Vogel's donut shop to buy day-old donuts to have something to eat. We called my sister Mary *"The General"* because she ensured that no one took more than their fair share. Between Mary and I, we ensured that all of us kids had something to eat when we could.

We were living in poverty but went to Catholic school because our wealthy Aunt Meme paid for us to attend. The nuns were strict and had no love for us Harringtons. We were known as the troublemakers. It didn't help matters that I struggled in school. Between the stigma of being the poor kid and feeling dumb, I was too ashamed to ask for help; instead, I became the tough guy and acted out. Let me tell you; I felt the sting of a ruler across my hand more than once. In the fifties and sixties, no one knew about ADHD or dyslexia (later in life, I learned that I had both). Instead, they labeled you as a problem and tried to discipline the devil out of you.

Being good Catholics, every Sunday, we went to Mass. Aunt Meme would pick up our grandmother and us for church. After church, she'd bring us back to her house for breakfast. She'd cook us eggs and bacon or sausage, which was a massive deal because we never got that kind of food at home. Sometimes, she'd take us for a drive after breakfast and buy us an orange crush or an ice cream. These are some of the best memories of my childhood. Aunt Meme was a special lady.

Basketball and Tornados

I never liked basketball, but since we had a hoop in our backyard, the neighborhood boys would come over to shoot baskets and hang out every Sunday afternoon. They liked to tease me because I didn't enjoy the game. They would call me "*Patty*" and things like that, standard kid stuff. More often than not, I'd just play with them to get them off my back.

I will never forget Palm Sunday, 1965; we were playing basketball like normal when suddenly everything became eerily quiet. Then all hell broke loose! The wind started howling, baseball-sized hale began to hurl down, and torrential rain came down in thick, dark sheets. Tornados began touching down throughout the city. We scattered and ran back to our houses as quickly as possible until the skies cleared. It scared the tar out of us, that's for sure! The storm took down the power lines in Indiana and the surrounding states; we were without power for several days. I later learned that my Dad was driving when the storm hit. A tornado picked up his car and threw him around a bit. His guardian angel was working overtime that day because my Dad walked away from the car without a scratch!

Family Secrets

My parents eventually separated for good and got a divorce when I was nine. However, the chaos continued. Mom would sometimes have Dad thrown into jail for not paying child support. So he would have to sneak into town and lay low to see us.

Dad would have us when mom went off on one of her benders or ended up back inpatient at the mental hospital. He would take us to the Holiday Inn, where we loved to swim in the swimming pool. Daddy Man O' Fats would buy us burgers and play around with us. We all loved those times with him. But my Dad also had a dark side to him. I learned years later that he had sexually abused all my sisters. That shame and trauma stained our entire family.

I was also molested when I was young, but not by anyone in our family. My father later told me that he assumed I would become a "*queer*" because of the abuse, which was how his generation thought about it. That wasn't what happened, though. My motor gets revved up for women. It always has.

Life continued despite our dysfunction. I hung out with friends, got into mischief, and went to work. I didn't become a pin boy but had various jobs from an early age. One of my first jobs was riding on a Sutter's milk truck, helping Charlie the milkman deliver milk. I can still feel myself tossed around the big, boxy milk truck every time we hit a bump or took a turn. Seatbelts were not even a thought back in those days. I'm amazed I didn't go home covered in bruises from the rough daily ride. One morning, the milk truck was in an accident, and I was hurt. Though I don't know it for a fact, I'm pretty sure I broke my tailbone. After that, the company made a policy against kids working in the milk trucks. That was the end of my short-lived career as a milk delivery boy!

Charlie was an old family friend. As cliché as it may sound, Charlie was also quite the ladies' man. Despite being married to my mom's best friend, he and my mom had an affair, which they didn't bother hiding from me. I learned a lot from Charlie. Things like "*it's okay to cheat on your wife or girlfriend,*" and I should *"be the man of the house"* once my Dad left. He spent a lot of time drilling that last one into my head. Instead of being a regular and carefree kid, I became saddled with all the responsibility and worry of being "*the man of the house*" at nine or ten years old. The problem was that even though I felt the weight of our dysfunctional family upon my frail shoulders, there was not much I could do to fix our problems. I was just a kid with the weight of the world resting upon him.

Although my father didn't touch me inappropriately, there was a level of sexual abuse in our relationship. When I was sixteen, I went on the road to help him sell aluminum siding. We always ended our day at a bar for a few drinks and something to eat. One night, after dinner, he hired a prostitute. When we returned to the hotel, he told her to let me have a go first. He watched us while we had sex, and then he took his turn with her while I was still in the room. It took me many years to get past the shame of that experience. It took even longer to acknowledge it was a form of sexual abuse.

Around that same time, my Dad remarried. His wife was always flirting with me and making suggestive comments. One evening while drunk, she went beyond flirting. She started touching me sexually despite my very clearly not wanting her attention. I told her no, pushed at her, and tried to get away, but she was a large woman and climbed on top of me, pinning me. Luckily, my Dad walked in as she was assaulting me. He threw her off me, smacked her around a bit, and told her to leave me alone. The trauma and shame of repeated sexual abuse were more secrets I needed to drink to forget. Those are the kind of secrets that try to claw their way up from your gut if you don't do something to push them back down.

CHAPTER THREE

Interview

K ristine:

My heart broke as Patrick told me about his early childhood. In my mind's eye, I could see him as a little boy dressed as a cowboy who wanted nothing more than to feel protected, provided for, and safe. I wished I could go back and rescue that child from the hard road ahead. But, no matter how much we want to, we cannot undo the past. From the present, I could only ensure that the little boy's voice was heard.

I wanted to hear the perspective of Patrick in those early years from those who knew him best, his siblings. Sadly Mary had passed, but his sister Lora and brother Mike were willing to share their experiences as his siblings in those early years.

Interview with Lora Buche

I first spoke with Patrick's sister Lora on a sunny, warm day in February 2020. I found her to be a warm, friendly lady who cares deeply for her brother and their family. She graciously shared her perspectives on Patrick, their growing-up years, and the effects of generational trauma.

Lora: *"As you probably already know, our childhood was chaotic. Patrick and I are what they call Irish twins. We were born only eleven months apart. However, he seems to have a better memory than I do,"* she laughed as if letting me in on an inside joke.

"I don't have many clear memories of our time in the orphanage or when Patrick was a young child. My aunt described him as a charming, sweet boy who was always on the go. I remember him as rambunctious, active, and always busy before we were teenagers. He wasn't mean, just really hyper. He always seemed friendly and outgoing. He made friends easily. A cute little boy, for sure." She pauses to gather her thoughts.

"Our parent's addictions and relationships affected all of us to our core. It was complete craziness. You never knew what was happening at any given moment. Did Dad have a job? Was Mom going to finger paint with us or be drunk and out of control? But even though crazy stuff was happening around us, we all still loved our parents and just wanted to be loved by them. I think Patrick had a closer relationship with Dad than the rest of us. I know they had a good relationship once Patrick was an adult. My Dad lived with him for a while, and they spent a lot of time together, more than I ever did. But that had much to do with other things that happened with my Dad and me."

"It was clear our mother and Patrick had a more complicated relationship for many years. Their relationship did improve significantly after he got sober. Around that time, we all (all the siblings) visited Mom and spent time with her. On that

trip, she finally told us her story. She opened up about all her abuse and trauma that led to her addictions and mental issues. Her father had sexually abused her and her sisters for years, and then she was raped by her teacher. She had a lot of trauma as a child and throughout her life. I think it was after that, that her relationship with Patrick began to heal.

However, there is no doubt that our parents' behavior significantly affected us growing up. They were rarely home; when they were, they fought violently or ignored us completely. Often they couldn't afford food or just forgot to buy it. Our clothes were ratty. If we wanted them washed, we had to do it ourselves. It was very dysfunctional.

Our parents did some crazy stuff, and we ended up in an orphanage. I think that affected Patrick more than me, as I was only two years old. I believe our time in the orphanage still haunts him.

With our parents, we had to love them anyway; we had to love them through it. It was rough because of some of the things that they did. I still have memories, as I'm sure Patrick does, where I think, "How could they do that to us?" But they did. They didn't physically abuse us but were busy fulfilling their needs. So they neglected us, ignoring our most basic needs, like ensuring we had food.

There was a lot of addiction on their part. I know Patrick went down that road and was an addict for a while. Looking back, I think it was only a short period but intense. I guess it started with him wanting to be like my Dad. Dad had that small-time mob kind of thing going on."

"I spent a lot of time researching our genealogy. I knew that our Dad had been orphaned and raised by extended family. However, I was surprised to learn that his mother was also orphaned and adopted. The cycle of abandonment, unintentional

though it was, seems to have repeated for several generations, as did the pattern of sexual abuse." Her voice is steady, but I can hear the lingering pain and sadness.

"Dad molested my sisters and me, despite mom's best efforts to protect us. Years later, Mary and I forgave him after working through the abuse and beginning to heal. It helped us to view him differently when we realized that some sexual abuse had also happened to him, though he never spoke of it. People from his generation didn't talk about those kinds of things.

He deeply regretted what he had done to us and his parenting choices. As adults, when we would get together as a family, tears would flow down his face, even though he never said a word. After a few minutes, he would get himself under control enough to participate in the family celebrations."

Interview with Michael Harrington

Michael Harrington is a busy businessman running his videography business. However, he didn't hesitate to speak with me about Patrick. From the beginning of the conversation, it was clear that though their relationship has had the usual ups and downs of all brothers, Mike greatly respects Patrick.

Michael Harrington: "I am the youngest of the four older siblings, so I don't remember much about the early years. To be honest, we weren't close during those early years simply because of our age differences. As the youngest, they mostly teased me, like older siblings do, because I needed the most attention.

Our younger years were hard because we were raised by two parents who were ill-equipped to care for six kids, financially or in any other way. Pat and Mary did look after us quite a bit, but we all had to learn to survive on our own. I remember washing my clothes at ten or eleven because I wanted to be clean when I went to school. If I wanted lunch, I would search the alleys for bottles and cans to turn in for a little change. It was the same for Mary, Pat, and Lora.

Our wealthy aunt paid for us to go to Catholic school. It wasn't easy because we were judged and looked down on in school. Everyone knew we were the poor Harringtons with a divorced mother (and all the other rumors around town about our parents).

The nuns were often cruel to us because they knew precisely whose family donated to the school, how much they gave, and that our parents weren't among them. We were just a drain on their resources.

I remember going to school in Pat's hand-me-down clothes. The pants were too big for me, and I didn't have a belt, so I had to walk around with my hands in my pockets all day to keep them from falling around my ankles.

One time Lora was being bullied in class and was crying. Pat learned about the teasing and called us all together for a family meeting. He has always had a bit of a temper and was hot under the collar about her being bullied. He said, "If this happens again, I will show up at your classroom door, and we are leaving school!" I was in third grade when that happened. Sure enough, one day, he was at my classroom door, and we all walked out of the school. So we did stick together as a group because we had to. No one else was going to look out for us.

Pat always ensured we were cared for and had food to eat. I respected and looked up to him because I. knew he would always do right by and protect us.

Recreating Patrick

Pat looked after a lot of people. For example, he had this friend Ron Boucher. Ron was the poorest kid in town, from the wrong side of the tracks. In other words, he was just like us, only worse off. Pat would sneak him into our garage to sleep because he needed a place to hide to avoid his parents' beatings.

I would wake up for school every day and scrounge something for breakfast. Then I would say goodbye to mom as she left for the factory, where she made $85 a week. Then I would eat whatever I'd managed to find in the kitchen. That was my routine.

But when Ron stayed the night, by the time I made it back to the table, Ron snuck out of the garage (our mom didn't know he was there), grabbed my breakfast, and ate it." Mike paused to laugh at the memory.

"This kind of thing happened all the time. Ron was a large part of my and Pat's lives for many years. Though he was closer to Pat than me."

"Pat has two very distinct sides to his personality. He is protective and caring and will give even a stranger the shirt off his back. But there is the nose to the grindstone, no-nonsense businessman that has created a successful business through sheer determination, a steely will, and hard work. Most people only see one side or the other. Very few get to see Patrick in all his complexity." Mike gathered his thoughts for a moment.

"I have two memories that I want to share that really show who Pat was while we were growing up.

When Pat was maybe fourteen or fifteen, he got a job at a hamburger stand. He took that job for us to have food (he'd bring home the cold fries and burgers at the end of his shift). But he also wanted to work so the rest of us would have Christmas presents under the tree. That was the best Christmas that I remember from my childhood. He was always doing things like that. He made sure we were okay, no matter what he had to do.

The second memory that stands out to me was when Pat was maybe fifteen. Pat was always a big guy, tall and broad through the shoulders. He was out working or running around with his friends when all hell broke loose at home. My oldest sister, Mary, had decided she was old enough to run her own life now that she was sixteen and started dating the town bad boy. My mom came home, drunk and mad, yelling, "You aren't ever going to see that boy again!"

Like any sixteen-year-old girl, Mary was screaming right back at her, "Yes, I am! And there is nothing you can do about it!" You know, the typical back and forth between a teen girl and her mom, except our mom was drunk.

Well, Pat walked into the house while they were in the middle of this nonsense. He didn't say a word. He just picked up our mom and put her on top of the refrigerator. That was the end of the argument. Everyone was laughing too hard to fight about anything after that. That was a typical Patrick move."

CHAPTER FOUR

The Path

"I always told my friend's not to talk about the good old days because we were living the good old days right then and there."

- Patrick Harrington

In Albany, near Marion, there was a dirt trail down to the river that everybody naturally called The Path. My buddies and I would ride our bikes down that path as fast as we could and then hang out by the river, just living easy. We lived a sort of Huck Finn and Tom Sawyer kind of life, floating in and out of trouble on the river. Overall, it wasn't a bad way to learn about nature's joys and healing properties.

Sometimes my cousin and I would launch a canoe and float along the Mississinewa, carrying the boat around the rapids, though calling them "rapids" might have been a bit of a stretch. At certain times of the year, the Mississinewa was more like a stream than a river. Still, it provided a real wilderness adventure for us and generations of Indiana boys like us.

Though one such adventure, I could have done without. My cousin and I liked to follow the train tracks, just walking and goofing around. One afternoon, we crossed a train trestle about 15 feet above the water. Suddenly, I was flying through the air straight into the water. I was terrified, sure that I would die! To this day, I have no idea what happened. One minute I was on the tracks; the next, I was flying through the air. Once I hit the water, I fought to the surface and sputtered, trying to breathe. I was able to swim to a beaver pond and wait for help. I still don't know if I tripped or if my cousin jokingly shoved me. It was the first time I looked death in the eyes, which was horrifying!

Sometimes we would sneak onto private land and fish in a pond there. We would take along a bunch of Swisher Sweets cigarillos, a longtime favorite of all the cool kids, and we'd smoke, fish, and daydream. Sometimes we would track rabbits and shoot one or two with a pellet gun, but mostly we were outside because it was a peaceful and relaxing place. When I was outside on an adventure, the craziness of my family life seemed far away, and I could be a regular kid just hanging out with my friends.

On one occasion, I decided to hang out on *The Path* alone. I wanted to get away and have an adventure by myself. Somewhere along my hike, I found a cute little kitten. I carried it around for a while, exploring and wandering with no real destination in mind.

We came to a bridge, and I carried the kitten across. To this day, I honestly don't know what came over me; I didn't have a plan when I started across the bridge. But once I got halfway across, I was overcome with the urge to drop that little kitten over the side of the bridge and watch it swim to shore. So I did. I ran across the bridge, down the bank, and grabbed the drenched, frightened kitten. Then I climbed back up to the bridge and did it again and then a third time. The last time I dropped it, the kitten didn't come up from the water to swim to the shore. I was confused and ashamed of what I had done. I didn't understand why I would do that to the poor little guy. I liked him. Why would I hurt him? At this moment, I learned how to keep a secret out of shame. You are only as sick as your secrets; my sickness was only beginning.

Riots and Popsicles

The fact that my family was poor was never a secret. My mother was "in the system," meaning she got financial help like cheese and food boxes from the government. It mortified me that our family got welfare.

I wanted to be more, to make something of myself. However, my siblings and I were mostly left to figure things out independently without healthy role models. Our parents were too focused on their individual needs and lives. The little direction I got from my Dad's example was not always a good influence.

My Dad always ran around with his small-time gangster friends, scheming one minor felony or another. But they did it in style, dressed in a suit and tie, with the pinky ring, the whole nine yards. This criminal world was what I was born into, the life experience I intimately knew. It was no surprise to anyone when I began down the same path. I don't even remember when I started selling drugs or stealing beer and cigarettes.

By the time I was eighteen, I had been in jail eight times, primarily for small-time hoodlum stuff like getting drunk, fighting, or telling off the cops.

We used to hang out at a local waffle house. Being teen guys, we'd get loud and obnoxious, and the manager would invariably call the cops. I would mouth off to one of them, and off to jail I'd go. Eventually, I learned that I might not ought to do that. I wouldn't end up in jail if I just didn't say anything. Ah, the lessons of youth.

I was a kid growing into a man without any healthy role models to emulate. Instead, I ran the streets with friends in the same family situation, and we figured it out the best we could. It wasn't all bad. I made some great friends. Friends like Ron Boucher and John Baxter, who I am still friends with today. Junior Jones and Mike Strictland didn't make it long enough to enjoy our golden years.

Ron was a big part of my life. Ron's home life was even worse than ours. Many nights I would sneak him into our garage so he could sleep somewhere safe, away from the beatings he got at home. Ron and I were inseparable for many years.

Now Junior Jones was one of my best buddies. We called him "Sticky Fingers" because he liked to steal stuff. We'd go to the store, steal a pack of underwear or something. Then we'd return it and get the cash for it. Of course, eventually, the stores caught on.

But Junior Jones was the best of us at stealing stuff. He even stole a T.V. once. He just walked right out with it. I still have no idea how he did it! We did all kinds of crazy shit together. Then I moved away, he married, and we continued our lives.

Years later, when I returned for my Dad's funeral, Junior was in the middle of getting a divorce. I saw him, and we caught up. Then I didn't hear from him again, but I did get a call from the cops. They asked if I had heard from Junior or knew where he was. I told them I didn't, but I wouldn't tell them even if I did. It was then that I learned Junior was wanted in connection with the killing of his wife. I repeated that I didn't know where he was. But I would bet they'd find him in a field dead if I were going to guess.

Sure enough, that's precisely where they found him. He had killed himself in a cornfield shortly after killing his wife. They had adopted two kids. So the kids lost both of their parents. I don't know what happened in their marriage except the little Junior told me when I visited for my Dad's funeral. That was a hard time for me. First, I lost my Dad. Then, Junior killed himself before I even got home from Dad's funeral.

But we raised hell back in those early days and had a great time doing it. We would hang out around the neighborhood pub and wait for the beer truck to arrive. While the driver was inside, we would swipe one of the cases of beer and hide it in the brush until the coast was clear. When it was safe, we would return to grab it and head off to the reservoir or out to a field to drink it.

I was about twelve when I started hard-core drinking because I had to. I needed to feel that buzz to get through life. Addiction got its ugly fangs sunk into me young. I wouldn't shake free of its hell-hound jaws for many years. By the time we were sixteen, the driver would just sell us a case or two off the back of the beer truck behind Don's Tap. It wasn't legal, but the driver made some cash on the side, and we weren't stealing it. All in all, it was a win/win situation for everyone. After we bought the beer, we'd hop into a 1963 Chevy, blast rock and roll, pound a few beers, and enjoy the easy life.

Years later, when I was on leave from the military, I was only nineteen and couldn't drink. But if I wore my dress uniform, they would allow me to drink in any bar. My buddy Danny Walls would come get me and say, "Patrick, put on your uniform, and we will go to Don's Tap and drink." The last thing I wanted to do was wear my dress uniform while on leave. "Nah, I don't feel like wearing my uniform."

"Just throw on your jacket, and they'll let you in." So I put on my uniform jacket, and we'd go drinking at the bar I used to steal beer from all those years before.

We would do all kinds of crazy stunts. One of the guys and my favorite things to do was to hang out at the reservoir with our girls. We'd break into the snack stand and chow down on chips and popsicles. I think we lived on popsicles that summer. I have to laugh at the thought of the poor sap who owned the snack stand having to restock it multiple times a week after our illicit late-night popsicle feasts.

On another escapade, we broke into an ice cream shop and stole all the ice cream. Man, we had to eat it all that night before it melted. We had ice cream coming out of our ears when the sun rose, but we got the job done!

Then there was the time we broke into the bowling alley to rob the vending machines. That adventure didn't go so well. I ended up in jail for that one.

Even with all the shenanigans, I always had a job. When I was fourteen, I worked at a hamburger joint named Meyer's Thrifty Chef. My co-workers sarcastically nicknamed me Speedy Gonzales because I

was so slow. It wasn't long before I got faster, but the nickname stuck. I worked as many hours as they would give me. When I got off work, I would bring home hamburgers and stale fries for my sisters and brother. When you are poor and hungry, you are grateful for whatever food you can get and don't complain about how stale it is. Poverty is more than a lack of money. It changes something fundamental in your personality. Once you've gone hungry or without electricity or water, you learn to get creative and find ways to never go without again. Experts have proven that extreme poverty gives people PTSD (post-traumatic stress disorder) for years, even after they are no longer impoverished. I have found this to be true in my life. To this day, I always have money socked away to be sure we will not go without food or the essentials. In my head, I know that we are in no danger of living in poverty, but there are some lessons learned early in life that can never be unlearned.

I ran around, getting into mischief, drinking, getting high, and dealing small-time drugs during my early teens. Despite it all, I still had an innocence about me. Life had dealt me some hard knocks, but for the most part, I had managed to skate through with minor scrapes and bruises. Between sixteen and seventeen, four significant events happened that stripped me of the rest of my naivete.

Mike Strictland was one of my closest friends. From the time I moved to Marion, we were inseparable. Whether stealing beer off the back of the delivery truck, hanging out at the reservoir, skipping school, or cruising the town, Mike was right there by my side. Mike had a way about him; he was the quintessential cool guy right down to the motorcycle he rode.

The last time I spoke to him, Mike and I made plans to skip school the next day, pick up two pretty girls that went to the Catholic school, and spend the day having fun. Sadly, that would never happen. I went to bed looking forward to hanging out with my friend and woke up the next morning to the news that Mike had died.

They told me he had been in a horrendous car accident. He had not survived; his silver cord was cut after sixteen short years. The accident had been so brutal that having an open casket for the viewing or funeral was impossible. I was utterly devastated. He was the first in what would become a long line of friends that I would outlive.

Mike's death shattered me. I remember my guilt as I stood by his closed casket at his funeral. Would it have made a difference if I had been with him that night? Would he have survived to see his seventeenth birthday? I don't know the answers to those questions. Time has taught me that it does no good to second guess the past. However, all these years later, I still miss Mike.

The loss of Mike was devastating. But his death was not the only loss I experienced that year; I also lost my first serious crush.

Annita was one of the most incredible and kind people I had ever met. My life didn't have a lot of kind and gentle souls in it. She never treated me as less than everyone else at school. She didn't make fun of me or tell anyone when she realized I didn't know how to read. Instead, she sat with me every day on the stoop of the school building and taught me how to read.

The nuns learned about our friendship and did everything they could to discourage it. They made it known that I was not good enough for her. I was just one of those "good for nothing" Harringtons. When separating us didn't work, the nuns told Anita's parents about our friendship and that I was a bad influence. Her parents then sent her to live with her grandmother. Though she eventually returned to school, the nuns kept a close eye on us. We weren't even allowed to speak to each other.

I had a lot of resentment toward the nuns for how they treated me. She represented a chance at something good in my life, and they ripped her away from me. Their treatment of me confirmed everything I already thought about myself; I was unworthy. I was damned determined never to be that poor, rejected kid again. I would find a way to be worth something, come hell or high water.

Years later, while attending a high school reunion, I saw Anita across the room and immediately flashed back to being that kid again. It didn't matter that I owned a successful business, had traveled the world, and was married to an amazing woman. At that moment, I was Pat Harrington, the kid who wasn't good enough to put away the tricycles in the orphanage; the poor boy, from the wrong side of the tracks, with a divorced mom and not enough food to eat, the boy the nuns said was unworthy of even being her friend.

I avoided her for most of the night. However, she saw me and kindly grabbed my hand. "You must remember me," she said. I told her I did, and we chatted for a few minutes and exchanged Facebook information, and then I escaped.

A few more years passed before she contacted me again. This time to send her condolences on my sister Mary's passing. My therapist encouraged me to tell her how she had affected my life. After a few days, I nervously sent her a Facebook message. She responded, and we started to message back and forth. She told me about her husband, her children, and her life in general. I then told her how much her kindness had meant to me all those years ago. She had been one of the few people who had seen something good and worthy in me; I will always be grateful for that. The conversation brought closure and healing to a deep, painful wound I'd carried in my soul for a long time.

After losing Mike and any chance of a friendship with Anita, I began to act out even more than before. It wasn't unusual for me to get arrested for mouthing off to a police officer or doing something young and stupid. Usually, I was sent to the local jail and then let go.

However, they decided to teach me a real lesson and sentenced me to the juvenile detention hall. It was a miserable place that I hated with a passion. My last straw was when the detention officers caught me smoking and cut off my hair as punishment. I was busting out of there! I called my good friend John Baxter and told him to wait for me down the road from the detention center. When the time was right, I used my toothbrush handle and escaped.

A fierce snow and ice storm swirled around me the night I broke out. I hadn't planned for the cold, escaping wearing only a thin t-shirt, jeans, and a pair of socks. I ran down the road, shivering, looking for John's car, but it was nowhere to be found. Later I found out that our wires had somehow gotten crossed. He had shown up at a different time, and I wasn't there. Freezing and miserable, I cut across a field and made my way to the closest phone I could find. I must have looked pitiful; wet, shivering, and in sopping wet socks. I found a phone and called John, who picked me up and hid me until my Dad could get me. Dad lived in Ohio then, but he drove all night to Indiana, picked me up, and brought me back to Ohio to live with him. It was a miserable night, but my escape became the stuff of legends!

While living with him, we worked together in Ohio, going door to door trying to sell aluminum siding. The aluminum siding racket toed the line of being a scam. So it was the perfect gig for my Dad. Watch the movie Tin Men starring Richard Dreyfus and Danny DeVito, to understand what it was like. It is a great movie. Every time I see it, I think of my Dad.

During this time, my Dad's new wife assaulted me. However, it wasn't all bad. My new "stepmom" had a sister around ten years older than me. Once I turned eighteen, she and I began an on-again-off-again affair for several years. Let me tell you, you can't buy the kind of education I got from her! Recently I ran into her, and she was in her eighties! How does that happen?.

I lived with my Dad for the rest of that year. When I was seventeen, I returned to Indiana and enrolled in Marion Public High School. Boucher, John, and most of my other friends already attended school there. So I had a close-knit group of friends ready and waiting when I started.

Indiana had a long history of segregation and racial tension. In 1930, Thomas Shipp, Abram Smith, and James Cameron were arrested for the robbery and subsequent shooting of Claude Deeter. Claude later died from the injuries he sustained. Mary Ball was with Deter when he was robbed. Ball claimed that the men also raped her though she later admitted that she lied about being raped.

On August 7, 1930, a mob of 15,000 white men and women broke into the Marion County jail, where the men were held until trial. They  beat all three men nearly to death and then hung Thomas Shipp and Abram Smith on the large tree outside the courthouse. James Cameron, who was only sixteen years old at the time, narrowly escaped with his life. The photograph of Thomas Shipp and Abram Smith hanging from the courthouse tree inspired the song *Strange Fruit*, written by Abel Meeropol and made famous by Billie Holliday. This atrocity was one of the inciting events that contributed to the protests and violence of the 1960s.

When I returned to Marion to attend high school in the fall of 1968, racial tensions were a powder keg, ready to explode with the slightest spark. That spark came on Friday, November 15. At 55 degrees, it was a perfect, sweater-wearing fall day. The morning passed in the monotony of an average high school day. Then in the cafeteria, all hell broke loose; punches and chairs started flying between the black and white students, seemingly without cause. However, I knew exactly what had happened to cause the mele.

Thursday, the day before the school burst into a race riot, my friends and I stood outside the school building, shooting the breeze and trying to impress our girls. We were typical teenage boys, young, dumb, and full of myself, as they say.

We'd been at it for a few minutes when a black boy who went to school with us came up and joined our conversation. He was nice enough, but then he started talking to one of the girls in our group. That was unheard of in those days. Black guys did not speak to white girls. To make it even more intense, the girl he was chatting with was my friend's girlfriend. Needless to say, he was pissed. In no uncertain terms, my buddy told the guy to shove off and leave his girl alone. Then the bell rang, we broke up, and returned to class. I had a gut feeling that the incident wasn't over; I knew the shit would hit the fan.

Friday, my buddy approached the flirty black guy and punched him during lunch. With racial tensions in the entire state nearing a breaking point, that single punch from a territorial boyfriend started an hours-long riot.

The riot started in the cafeteria and quickly spilled out into the hallways. As the punches started flying, I picked up my sister Lora and my girlfriend, one under each arm. I carried them like footballs outside, away from the danger.

Then I balled up my fist, headed back into the cafeteria, and started throwing down. All I had to defend myself were my fists and a fork, but I wasn't one to abandon my friends in the middle of a fight. It got intense, everyone using whatever they could grab as a weapon. Then the shop guys brought 2x4s into the mix, and things went from bad to worse.

Eventually, the police were called in and arrived to end the riot. After a few hours, the mayhem was over, leaving blood, bruises, and an ever-widening racial divide in its wake.

Because of the racial aspect, the FBI came in to investigate. But I refused to speak when they tried to take my statement. I had no use for snitches then and still don't, as far as that goes.

The Start of a Terrible Relationship

Although I had been drinking since I was twelve and using recreational drugs for years. I was a bonafide alcoholic by sixteen. I had to have some kind of booze to make it through my day. At my young age, I already carried too many secrets, pain, and sorrow that needed to be pushed down until I couldn't feel them. Alcohol was my emotional anesthesia. I smoked a lot of pot, dropped acid, and dabbled in mushrooms. But my drug of choice was alcohol; it quickly became my best friend. I would have to drag myself to work every morning, feeling like crap, but by the time the night came around, I would feel better. I'd hang out with my friends and start drinking again. The next day, I'd be dragging into work, looking and feeling like crap, and the whole process started again. It was an endless cycle.

Of course, I now know that alcohol is loaded with sugar, which is a depressant. Between the unbalanced hormones of puberty and some pretty extreme trauma and abuse, I was already depressed and struggling with suicidal ideations. The drinking only made that depression worse after the buzz was gone.

By the time I was driving, I would get blackout drunk regularly. It was normal for me to drive the country roads drinking until I ran out of gas. I would leave the car where it was and stumble back home. Later, once I sobered up, I couldn't remember where I left the car, so my friends would drive me around the back roads looking for it.

One night, when I was sixteen or seventeen, I ran out of gas and stumbled down the roadside when a car stopped, and some guys offered me a ride back to town.

We drove a few minutes before they attacked and tried to rob me. But they had picked the wrong mark because I didn't have a dime. They were unimpressed when they learned I was dead broke.

Even in my drunken state, I could tell this would not end well. I've never been one to patiently wait until I'm attacked when there is a fight in the air, especially when I'm outnumbered! So I grasped my mostly empty beer bottle by the neck and smashed it over the head of a guy sitting next to me!

Then I got into it with the other guy in the back of the car. I jumped out of the moving vehicle while they were driving through an addition (we called housing communities additions back then). The driver slammed on the brakes, backed up, and all four guys piled out to come after me. I managed to hold my own against the first two guys, but once the third and fourth guys joined, they had me on the ground. They beat me up pretty good, kicking me repeatedly, especially in the head.

When I came to, I somehow made it to a nearby house. They called the cops and brought me to the hospital, where they kept me because I had a severe concussion. Drinking was already having severe consequences in my life.

A Trip to Remember

As I mentioned before, psychedelics and I never got along. One night my buddy and I were doing mushrooms and driving around higher than kites. Suddenly, we came to a roadblock swarming with cops and drug dogs. I was flipping out, scared out of my mind. I knew there was no way we were getting out of this mess without going to jail, so I began to take off my shoes and socks.

My friend asked, *"Man, what the hell are you doing?"*

I responded, *"If I'm going to jail, I'm not going while wearing these damn shoes and socks!"*

"Going to jail? Man, what are you talking about?" My buddy was confused.

"Look at all the cops and dogs! There's no way we aren't going to jail tonight!"

"Dude, there are no cops and dogs. You're having a bad trip," My friend laughed.

I had hallucinated the whole thing! Yeah, psychedelics were never really my thing.

CHAPTER FIVE

Interview

K ristine:

The world that Patrick grew up in is simultaneously foreign and familiar to me. I, too, grew up not always knowing if there would be food in the house and wearing ill-fitting hand-me-downs from the Salvation Army and kind-hearted church ladies. Poverty, I understand. However, I cannot fathom being a child completely neglected by unstable parents. In a world where severe mental illness and addiction have subverted the most primal parental instincts. A world where the gangster life is glamorized. Try as I might to understand it, the world of Patrick's youth is as foreign to me as the landscape of the moon. I interviewed his longtime friend, John Baxter, to better understand their teen years.

John Baxter Interview

It was a brisk February afternoon when I had the privilege of meeting John. His laughter was contagious as he recounted the youthful shenanigans that he, Patrick, and their friends got up to together. John's memory was like a steel trap. He remembered even the most minute details with clarity, humor, and at times, brutal honesty more than fifty years later.

His memories of racial tensions and riots of the sixties framed the issues from the perspective of someone who lived through them.

John: *"I met Patrick when I moved to Marion, Indiana, from Missouri, my sophomore year of high school. Our good friend Ron Boucher introduced us in 1969 or 1970.*

Pat came from a large family. I have always deeply admired him because he had a terrific work ethic. While the rest of us were playing around, he was working. What impressed me even more was that he worked to help his mom financially. He was always taking care of his sisters and brothers. Pat and I have been friends for fifty years. I guess you could say he was the one who inspired me early on to be a good person. But even while being responsible, Pat, Ronny, and I had a great time.

Oh boy, did we get up to some trouble back in those days!" John chuckled to himself for a moment before continuing. *"There was one summer we spent a lot of time hanging out at Salamonie Reservoir with our girls. We had a whole group that would be there almost every night.*

One night, we were hungry, and someone had the bright idea to break into the snack shack. After that, we lived on free popsicles and potato chips all summer!" John was laughing in earnest as he remembered those summer nights.

After a moment, he began again, "Then there was the time Patrick called me in the middle of the night from some hotel out on the bypass and asked me to come to pick him up. It was the middle of winter, maybe January or February. It was cold, and there was a lot of snow on the ground.

I pulled up to the hotel, and he got into the car. I did a double-take when I saw he wasn't wearing shoes or a coat.

I said, "Patrick, what are you doing?"

He shrugged and said, "I broke out of the detention center with my toothbrush," like it was nothing. He crossed the snow-covered cornfield between the detention center and the road in only his socks and a t-shirt. Patrick always was a tough son of a gun.

I graduated in '70, and Patrick didn't enter the service until '71. So Patrick and Ronnie got me a job working with them at Marion Malleable Iron Works. When I got my first paycheck, we headed out to celebrate with Nick Bushy. Nick ended up marrying Patrick's sister, Lora.

We were all at the drive-in, just hanging out and cutting up. But then Nick and I got into it over something; I don't even remember what it was. However, we were going at it pretty good, spraying each other's cars with beer, that kind of stuff. But then Nick crossed the line and tossed wine in my face. That was it! Patrick knew we were about to go at it hard. He stepped in. "Y'all can't fight here. You'll end up going to jail. I'll bring you over to the bowling alley parking lot. No one will be there."

He piled us into his car and drove Nick and me to the bowling alley, where we started to fight. The fight didn't last too long because I punched Nick and broke my own hand." John pauses to laugh at the irony.

"That ended the fight, and they drove me to the hospital to get the bones set. The next day Nick came by my place and apologized. We all came out of it as good friends. Patrick was always trying to keep the peace in our group.

Patrick and Ronnie talked to their boss, who transferred me to the shipping department where they worked. This allowed me to keep my job while my hand healed. The three of us had a genuine brotherly love for one another. It really hurt when Ronnie passed away a few years ago." John sighs. It is clear that he still feels the loss of Ron Boucher deeply.

"While working at the factory, Patrick got his own apartment on Poplar Street in Marion.

I was the only one with access to a pick-up truck because my Dad had a '69 Chevy I would drive. Late one night, Pat called and said, "Come get me. I need to get some furniture for my place." I got into the truck and headed his way. The whole drive, I was thinking, "Where the hell is he going to buy furniture in the middle of the night?" When I got to his place, Pat hopped into the truck and told me to head to the mobile home sales lot. I still had no idea what we were doing, but I had his back, whatever it was. Turns out he had decided to go "furniture shopping" for his apartment in their show home! We broke in and loaded up my truck with everything he needed! That is my favorite story about Patrick from those days. In those days, we used to get up to all kinds of mischief."

"After that, we lost touch for a while. During the draft, Pat's number was like number 2 or 3. My number was high enough that I was unlikely to get drafted. So Pat headed to the military. Not long after that, I got into trouble with the law, which

landed me in jail with a felony conviction. I served my time and then got married. After my felony, I couldn't go into the military.

On a bet, Ronnie asked out Alice Bell, who was worth millions. They ended up getting married. She was worth millions. Suddenly Ronnie Boucher, the poorest kid in town, was rich. They moved to Florida, and I worked for him at one of the shoe stores he had opened.

He was the best man at my wedding. Pat couldn't be there because he was in the military, stuck on base at the time.

Pat got really depressed about his circumstances during that time. He was down between the accident and the fact they wouldn't let him leave the base. I guess they kept him because of a gunfight with some black guys. But I didn't know about that until later. I thought they kept him on the base because he'd been in a bad motorcycle wreck.

After leaving the army, Pat also came to work for Ron Boucher. But he worked at his club in Miami. While I was still in Naples with my wife, working at the shoe store. I ended up having a falling out with Ronnie and moved to Wyoming. Pat and I never connected in Florida. I don't really know why. I guess life happened. Anyway, I remember that he and Ronnie parted ways shortly after I left, and Pat went to college."

"We didn't connect again until many years later when Pat found me on the Marion Giants High School alumni web page. He had his rug business going by that point. He and Olivia stayed at our place in Wyoming a few times. My wife and I went to their place as well. Pat took me out to fly falcons with him. That was a lot of fun.

Patrick Harrington

I also met him at a rug show in Scottsdale, Arizona. From the moment we got back in touch, it was like no time had passed. We took up like we never left off. He was the same kind-hearted person that he was in high school. I saw how much he had accomplished with his life. And, of course, I met his wife, Olivia, an amazing woman. Pat cares deeply about veterans because of his time in the military. And he would still give anyone the shirt off his back.

When we got back in touch, I finally told him I had always admired him because of his compassion for his family and mother. I love Patrick like a brother. I know that no matter what happens, he will always be there for me, no matter how much time passes. And I will always be there for him."

CHAPTER SIX

God and Country

"I have always been a loner. A man without a country."

- Patrick Harrington

I remember the moment I got the news that I was drafted, like a vivid snapshot in my head. It was 1969, and I was in bed with my girlfriend in my apartment. My buddies busted through the door and told me, "You're up." I didn't plan on joining the military, but I wasn't against the idea. I was happy to get out of town and start something new.

In 1971 they finally called me up. I did my basic training at Fort Knox in Kentucky. I was put in an old wooden barracks left over from WWII. They were hot in the summer and cold in the winter. Generations of soldier ssweated and shivered in those barracks.

Every day of boot camp was a living hell because I was in excruciating pain. The running and drills resulted in painful stress fractures in my heels and shins. They were desperate for soldiers. A little thing like fractured bones from training accidents wouldn't slow me down from my combat training. They drove me to our training and exercise sites in whatever supply truck was headed that way.

I had a lot of experiences while serving, and they forever changed me. When they had us go into the gas chamber to train us for exposure to tear gas on the battlefield, the sergeant would ask, "Does anyone have a cold? Well, you won't after this!" And boy, was he right! The gas evacuated everything in there. We all had snot and mucous going everywhere. It was probably the best thing I ever did for my sinusitis. It cleaned you right out!

Honestly, much of my time there was a damn shit show. I still have PTSD from some of the things I experienced on that base during my years there.

Danny

We would see pictures of the Vietcong's atrocities on our soldiers killed or captured. They cut the ears off of dead soldiers and kept them as trophies.

These pictures made me think of my good friend Danny Frankboner. Danny had been one of the guys I palled around with back in Marion, Indiana.

On December 7, 1969, Danny was killed in Bin Thuan, South Vietnam, by small arms fire. He was the 1000th soldier from Indiana killed in the Vietnam War. That still haunts me to this day, knowing *what he endured* while serving. My wife later helped me deal with his loss by reminding me that I needed to live my life the best I could for him and myself. Danny is one of the reasons I hand out chips to veterans when I see them, and I am sure to thank them for their service.

I was proud to learn the Grant County Vietnam Memorial has Danny listed among those killed in action. It is right that his name and sacrifice will be remembered by the generations to come.

I made it through boot camp by the skin of my teeth *though* I did not pass one PT test. But they passed me on. It was wartime, and they forged the documents. When he examined me, the Army doctor noted that I had severe sinusitis, chronic headaches, and stress fractures from falls and one-on-one combat training accidents.

I entered Advanced Individual Training (aka AIT) to become a cook (aka "a spoon") because of my health issues. It was an intense training experience that advanced my career as superintendent of my unit. I took a lot of pride in my job. I would get up at 03:30 to crack 30 dozen eggs. After I cooked them, I'd serve them from big containers in the mess hall or take them to the field. The military is a team; armies are stronger when their soldiers are well-fed. The army doesn't go anywhere without food or cooks.

Some people think, "You were just at Fort Knox. It's not like you served in Vietnam; you weren't in battle." I used to feel shame about that. I felt like I was somehow less of a soldier. But then I realized that what I did was important. It helped to prepare the guys to serve in Vietnam. I was an essential member of the team, even if I didn't go to war.

Guarding the Gold

While stationed at Fort Knox, we had nothing to do with the gold there. In 1971, while in AIT, my commander told me I was reassigned temporarily. They had hired local high school football players to load and

unload the 27-pound gold bricks. They were moving the gold for an audit and needed extra security. So I was on rover patrol with a bunch of other guys. We were put in the back of a canvas-covered truck with M-16s. Then we patrolled throughout the night for about two weeks. It was one of the coolest things I did while stationed at Fort Knox!

Crazy Times at Fort Knox

I saw all kinds of messed-up shit, like guys jumping off the roofs on the base or taking handfuls of pills and trying to kill themselves so they wouldn't have to go to Vietnam. I saw a hold-over trainee coming out of the latrine, stumbling around with a needle hanging from his arm. He was coming towards me and fell. I knelt down and picked up his head to see what was happening. He had a crazy grin and was sweating with a glazed look in his eyes. I laid his head down and ran to tell the first Sargeant. He told me to return to work, and they would take care of it. I never heard what happened to him, but I've had flashbacks about it ever since.

We were all kids. The military knows you can't tell a thirty-year-old to do some of this dangerous stuff. A thirty-year-old is going to say, "Hey, wait! That sounds dangerous. I don't  think I think we ought to do that." But you tell a bunch of eighteen and nineteen-year-olds, and they will just do what you tell them to do. They don't question it; they do it.

The military didn't document a lot of the crazy stuff we did. Now that I'm trying to get VA benefits for these things, the military shrugs and moves on because none of it was documented. For example, I have hearing problems because they never provided us hearing protection.

They told us to stick cigarette butts in our ears. If you see pictures of soldiers with cigarettes sticking out of their ears, now you know they weren't crazy; that was their hearing protection! The VA did eventually give me hearing aids. I'm very grateful for that.

The Fight that Changed Me

Racial tensions were still very high in the nation at this time. I was one of three white guys in a group of twenty soldiers. Needless to say, it was an uncomfortable situation. Mostly, I kept my head down and tried to get along, as they say. But I was never one to be pushed around. One of the black guys in my unit and I had some heated words over one thing or another. I honestly don't even remember what started the animosity between us. I assume it probably had something to do with drugs.

On the last night of AIT, he grabbed and assaulted me from behind while I was naked and coming out of the shower. He was also naked while he attacked me. We were slipping all over the wet floors as we went at it. But I managed to hold my own.

Then he was joined by a couple more soldiers, some still fully clothed, including their boots. I'd been in more than my fair share of fights in my life, but nothing compared to this. It was brutal; I was fighting for my life.

One guy kicked me with his boots, while another kicked me in the balls. All the while, the beating of my head and the rest of my body continued. There are things that happened to me during that assault that

I have only ever told my therapists, and they haunt me still. It will suffice to say that being naked while assaulted left me with no protection in even the most basic ways.

I was still fighting for my life when my attacker put a gun to my head, cocked it, and said, *"What are you going to do now?"* I remember the sound of that gun cocking like it was yesterday. It has haunted my dreams for fifty years. I said, *"You're the one with the gun. You tell me,"* They had me down, but I wouldn't beg. Soon after, I passed out but returned to consciousness as my attackers urinated on my face and the rest of my body. I don't know how long I drifted in and out of consciousness. I awoke beaten, naked, smelling like urine, and unsure how I made it to my bunk. I did not report this assault then because I was embarrassed, ashamed, and afraid of retaliation. From that horrible day on, I have always carried a gun. I don't go anywhere without at least one gun on me to this day. They eventually moved me to my own corner room in a new barracks. I padlocked the door but occasionally they would search it.

I don't know who reported the attack to our superiors. They came and asked me about what went down, and I refused to say a word. I have never been and will never be a rat. They gave me an ultimatum, either I testify at the trial of my attacker, or I would be confined to base for six months. Again I refused. As a result, I couldn't leave the base for six months, which added to my trauma.

I don't remember where I was or what I did over the several weeks following the assault. My therapists have told me that losing time is normal after experiencing trauma. It was the end of the AIT cycle, and I was assigned to a new duty station within Fort Knox. I immediately began to keep to myself, did not trust my co-workers, was scared, and had nightmares. I started to smoke cigarettes, and my drinking became even more out of control. I just wanted to escape the situation and repeatedly requested to be sent to Vietnam but was denied. For years I did not share what happened until I was encouraged by my support group to seek in-person therapy. In therapy, I began to do the work around the trauma. I was finally able to acknowledge the depth of my trauma.

The trauma affected my relationship with my girlfriend when I finally went home on leave. We had been close before my assault, but I was now completely shut down emotionally, could not communicate, drank heavily, and was always angry. I could not function sexually. I was unable to touch her and could not stand for her to touch me. The more she begged me to tell her what was happening, the more I shut her out. After a few visits, she broke up with me because I was no longer the same man she had fallen in love with. I was drowning in depression, anger, hopelessness, and self-loathing.

During leave, I discovered a guy living down the street from us exposed himself to my sisters as they walked past a construction site. He thought he was safe because I was away in the Army.

John was with me as I headed out to teach him a lesson. I was going to soak his car in gas and throw a match. But John convinced me that I probably better not ought to do that while I was in the Army.

Instead, I threw a brick through the big picture window of his house. I made sure he knew why he was paying for a new window. The cops never did a thing about it. Turns out they didn't like scum-bag perverts either.

I had a legitimate reason to want to hurt that sicko, but my need for violence was more a reaction to the assault. I was looking for reasons to hurt someone, anyone. When a person is assaulted, feeling powerless to stop what is happening to them is one of the hardest, most traumatizing things to overcome. I spent years overcompensating by wrapping myself in violence and secrecy.

On May 12, 1972, I awoke after having a terrible nightmare. In it, I ran with a gun in the dead of night away from the barracks, naked, trying to escape my attackers. The men hunting me were closing in, so I hid under a bush and brush. In my panic, I dropped the weapon and feverishly felt around for it as my attackers got closer and closer. As I saw the men's boots approaching, I was terrified that they had found my hiding spot. Luckily, my fingers felt the gun. I put it to my head and pulled the trigger. I would never let them get me again.

I awoke drenched in sweat and shaking. I hopped on my motorcycle and took off, trying to clear the remnants of the dream from my head. The nightmare had unnerved me and left me feeling like I had no way out. I was at a loss and didn't know what to do. I wanted all the nightmares, fear, depression, anger, and flashbacks to stop.

While still on the base, I began to drive as fast as my motorcycle could take me. I rounded a corner and aimed my bike at a bridge. I needed all the suffering to be over. Without a second thought, I drove full speed into the bridge in an attempt to kill myself.

When my head cleared, I realized I was injured and needed help. The bike was a mangled mass of metal, with the handlebars at 45 angles, and the footpegs were completely gone! I somehow made it back to my barracks by limping the bike along. I was taken to the base's ER.

The nurse that checked me in asked what was wrong. I said, "*I cut my penis.*" She did a double-take and immediately sent me back for treatment.

The doctor quickly came into the room. He examined me and filled a large syringe. Then he said, "*You are about to have the biggest erection you've ever had,*" and laughed. I don't remember how many stitches it took to stitch it back up, but it was a lot!

I healed up pretty well, but I have had continuing prostate issues caused by that wreck. Mostly, it made for a great drinking story back in the day.

I have been told that since I lost consciousness. My doctors now believe I received a traumatic brain injury (aka TBI) due to that accident. But back then, they weren't as worried about head injuries, concussions, and all that jazz. If you were conscious, they would tell you to take a few aspirin for the headache and be glad it wasn't worse. They didn't scan my head or brain because I regained consciousness and got to the hospital. As a result, I didn't learn about my TBI until much later. My psychiatrists believe this injury has caused some of my mental health problems.

PTSD is a real bitch. There is no cure, but there is treatment. I have spent a lot of time working through this trauma with my therapist. She is the one that pointed out that this was a type of sexual assault. My earlier abuse made this assault that much more traumatizing. Even in the military, I am a man without a country. I have PTSD from my military service, even though I never saw combat.

Hello My Old Friends: Drugs and Depression

I completed my six-month confinement and was granted leave. I returned to Indiana, bought as much weed as possible, and hitchhiked back to base. I wasn't supposed to keep a house off base, but I rented a stash house in the town where I kept the drugs. I also bought my orange 750 Honda motorcycle to quickly go between the base and town. I would ride that thing all over the place. I saw one not too long ago and realized how small that bike was. I don't know how I managed to ride it as tall as I am. But I loved that bike!

I would ride my motorcycle into town, hide the drugs on it, and head back to the base. One night, I had a horrible feeling before heading out. I've always had a sixth sense when it comes to danger. I don't know why, but I know it's kept me alive or out of jail many times over the years. I hid the drugs on my bike and left despite my gut feeling. I had only been on the road only a few minutes when I saw a bunch of cops and cop cars. My heart was pounding in my throat. I had no doubt that I would be arrested that night. The cops pulled me over and searched my bike for the drugs several times, but they didn't find them. I thanked the universe that I was a lucky S.O.B!

The military didn't help my mental state. I still had secrets and shame that needed to be pushed down and deep depression. I had struggled all my life with thoughts of killing myself. I would think, "*I could just drive off the road, and it would all be over,*" or "*I could put a bullet in my head, and this will all stop.*"

So Long, Kentucky! Hello, Florida!

Eventually, I was promoted to the Officer's Club as a chef. While there, I met General George Patton's son and grandson. By the time I was honorably discharged, I was a Spec 4 and had received a few ribbons.

I had a friend take what was left of the drugs and sell them out of state. But he ran off with the drugs, and I never saw him, the money, or the drugs again. Once again, I was broke, so when my friend Ron Boucher offered me a job in Miami, I was happy to accept the offer.

I didn't know anything about serving my country when I was drafted. They told me it was my time to serve, so I did. But now I understand, and my service means a lot to me. I am so glad I had the honor to serve. I speak with veterans everywhere I go. We have a common thread that binds us. We all served at different times and in different places, but we all served. We are a brotherhood like no other.

The day I was released from active duty, Ron Boucher came to pick me up in a limousine. I pulled off that base in style, heading to Florida to work for Boucher in his upscale *Tom Jones Supper Club*. Things were about to get real crazy.

CHAPTER SEVEN

From Miami to Albuquerque

"The devil wants me dead, but he will settle for drunk."

-Patrick Harrington

I left Fort Knox in that limo and never looked back. I was headed to sunny Miami, where the days were hot, and the parties were even hotter. At 20 years old, I was ready for the heat. I even looked the part dressed in my white jacket and patent leather shoes.

Despite being broke and working in the nightclub kitchen, I lived the high life in the penthouse at the top of the Coconut Grove Hotel. Ron took good care of his friends in that way. It wasn't long before I moved out of the kitchen and worked as a bartender making drinks for the rich and famous. For the first year or so, I loved living the high life. The unlimited drinks, drugs, and beautiful women were the stuff of most 20-year-old guys' fantasies. It also meant I didn't have to deal with any of the shit in the past. I could ride that endless party carousel and push everything else down deep.

Tom Jones Supper Club was a Miami hot spot. I talked motorcycles with Evel Knievel, met rock stars, and hung out with Miami's most beautiful dancing girls. But behind the glitz and the glamour, there was a dark underbelly to the club.

The rumor was Ron had connections to the New York mob. During the day, the feds would come in for lunch, and gangsters mingled with celebrities at night. It was almost surreal.

All the servers and valets were trained in martial arts and packing guns. As the bartender, I started carrying a .38 in a purple and gold velvet *Crown Royal* bag. That was my gun of choice until a retired cop turned valet told me about the Browning. *"This one guy had me pinned down. I was waiting for him to reload, but he just kept shooting. The damn gun never seemed to run out of bullets!"* The Browing was the first high-capacity gun you could buy. As soon as I got off work, I bought one. From that moment on, I always carried the Browning.

By 1973, I was running the club for Ron. I saw celebrities like *Tina Turner*. I served drinks to Miami's elite, keeping the club running as smoothly as possible while also trying to keep Ron from getting killed. As a 22-year-old fresh out of the military, it was as exciting as it was exhausting.

Ron Boucher fought all the same childhood demons I did, and some were uniquely his own. There were times he would lock himself in his luxury condo, high as a damn kite, and watch CNN all day and all night. At other times Ronnie was prowling Miami's hottest clubs for a quick hookup. He was a proper sexual deviant in every way. He and his wife had what would be called an open relationship in polite society.

Patrick Harrington

Often she would go to the clubs and scout girls for him. He was not shy about sharing her with other men, either. Honestly, the sexual escapades got old very quickly.

Ron loved all the vices, including gambling. Late one night, well, early morning technically, I got a call from my kid brother, Mike. Mike spent the summer in Miami with me, working at the club. He was worried because Ron lost five grand gambling with mobsters and didn't want to pay up. Needless to say, this was not going over well. Mikey was trying to talk some sense into a drunk and probably high Boucher, but that was going nowhere fast. He needed me to come and open up the safe to get the money. I ran to the club, ensured everyone received their money, and returned Ronnie to his condo. Life with Ron Boucher was never dull, that's for sure!

Around this time, Ron sent me out on the road with Red Foxx as his "manager." I set up his gigs and arranged the details, but my real job was the "*money man.*" The *big men* in New York demanded to be paid in cash. I will leave it to your imagination as to why that might be. The clubs paid us for the number of people who walked through the door. Needless to say, some club owners would try to pull a fast one and short-change you. I was there to make sure that didn't happen. Being a muscular six foot four, I would chuckle as grown-ass men hurried past me with fear in their eyes. I used that to my advantage while collecting the cash from the much older venue owners, who sometimes questioned why we would not accept checks. I was only 22 years old and handling up to fifty thousand dollars a night. That was more money than I had seen in my entire life up to that point! It was exhausting, but the experience served me well. A few years later, I opened my own music venue in Albuquerque.

Getting Schooled

The constant partying, cleaning up after Ron, and road life became too much. I was over the crap and drama.

I took a day off and headed to one of my favorite bars. It was a dark, quiet place in a basement. The kind of place serious drinkers go to do serious drinking. I spent the day getting shit-faced.

Then and there, I decided to quit the club. Boucher's instability and the dangerous things he was involved in were a recipe for disaster. Eventually, *Tom Jones Supper Club* burned to the ground; it was an open secret that the mob had ordered it.

Using my GI bill, I enrolled in Miami Dade Community College after I quit Boucher's club. They had an independent studies program for people with ADHD. It's incredible what a difference the right learning environment makes! My whole life, I had felt like a big dummy. School had been a demoralizing and torturous experience. But now, I knew the answers to the questions before the teachers even asked them. I chose to study business. And as it turned out, I was really good at business!

I also took some fun classes, like scuba diving and photography. Scuba diving was fun, but photography classes truly grabbed hold of me.

I have always relived my memories as a series of movie reels and snapshots in my mind. Movies had always been an escape from my inner demons. It made sense that photography would come naturally to me and become a lifelong passion.

It also came in handy as a drug trafficker. Camera equipment was a fantastic place to hide money and product! Being a photographer also provided me a great cover story. No one looks too closely at the guy in the shadows shooting photos of those in the spotlight. Life in obscurity always suited me just fine.

While in college, I carried my books around in an old gas mask slung over my shoulder like a purse. I don't know why. I just liked it. At 6'4 and in my prime, I was intimidating enough that no one dared say anything about it.! I was one cool  dude, riding around on my little orange Honda 750 motorcycle with my gas mask bookbag slung across my body.

But riding my bike in Miami traffic was quite a harrowing experience. It didn't help that I was usually wasted or close to it. I was still drinking and doping those demons away.

One night I was pulled over for one reason or another. The cop had to know I was wasted, but he said, *"You look tired."* *"I am. I just got off of work,"* I told him. *"Be safe,"* he said as he waved me on. But I was too wasted to be careful. That night I got into an accident that busted me up pretty good. I was laid up for a while from that. It took me years to admit that this "accident" hadn't been as accidental as I tried to convince myself. I had a death wish and was determined to find a way to make it come true.

I finished up my college experience with a 3.96-grade point average. I had struggled a bit with economics, and Algebra kicked my butt. However, the overall college experience was good for me, boosting my self-confidence quite a bit. I was not the dumb loser I had been told I was growing up.

California Dreaming

I was no longer a delinquent from Marion, Indiana, or a young recruit in Fort Knox. I had grown into my own man with a wealth of real-world experience. Florida had been good for me, but my feet were itchy. I hopped on my motorcycle, strapped my duffle bag to the back, bundled up because it was the middle of winter, and headed west to California.

It was not an easy trip. The chain kept slipping off of my bike every few miles. I'd have to stop and reattach it after it bounced off the road. It was also bone-chillingly cold, with strong winds that kept blowing me off the highway!

Then I hit a big snowstorm in El Passo, Texas. Who the hell would have guessed I'd hit snow in Texas? I had to hole up for the night and wait it out. But it only slowed me down for a day. The following day the sun came out, and the snow was completely gone! So I was back on the road, heading toward my bright future in the Golden State.

California

Ron Boucher and I hit the LA scene together. He'd decided to head out west, as well. Once again, I moved into his penthouse. This time it was on the Sunset Strip atop Tower Records, the most famous of all the Tower Record locations. I rubbed elbows with the biggest stars of music, television, and movies. Talk about living the high life!

One of the snapshots in my head is from the moment I arrived in LA. I was decked out in my jean jacket and a floppy jean hat, just strolling down Sunset Strip, checking out the acts at The Troubadour, Whiskey-A-Go-Go, and The Comedy Club. Man, I didn't know it then, but I lived in the middle of entertainment history as it was being made!

I worked at Victoria's Station Steakhouse as a rib carver but made my real money transporting drugs in one form or another. One of my main routes was running pot back and forth between LA and New Mexico.

While working at Victoria's Station, I met Connie. We started dating, and before too long, she was pregnant. When she had the baby, Connie wanted to be close to her family in Albuquerque. I knew I could find work because of my contacts as a drug runner. So we packed up and moved to New Mexico.

In 1976 my son Gabriel was born, and he was a chip off the old block, as they say.

CHAPTER EIGHT

Interview With Mike Harrington

Kristine:

Hearing Patrick's experiences is like dancing through the pages of 1970s history. He was at all the right places and times with all the right people, quietly observing watershed events from the shadows. I couldn't wait to hear more.

Knowing Mike was integral to Patrick's early days in New Mexico, I asked if he would talk to me again. He graciously agreed. Like his brother, Mike is a very charismatic man with a great sense of humor and a gift for storytelling.

Mike Harrington Take Two

"Pat and I had a lot of crazy times. However, we didn't hang out together during my younger years. I was the annoying little brother. Pat had his friends, and they got up to what they did. And I had my friends." He paused as if lost in memory before continuing, "From when I was 12 or 13 years old, I'd run out the door early in the morning and return home later that evening. I'd be damned if Mom knew what we were doing during that time. We'd break into factories for the hell of it. Or we would go up to Don's Tap House and rip off a case of beer from the delivery

truck. *The driver always brought four cases of beer into the bar. We'd run and grab the fifth case off the truck and hide it in the bushes until he was gone—just a bunch of crazy kid shit. I doubt Pat knew I was doing all of that."*

Mike sighs, "Pat had more of a relationship with Dad than I did. From when he was about 14 on, Pat would pull me aside and ask, "Hey, do you want to go see Dad?" By this time, Dad was pretty far out of the picture because every time he came into town, our mom would have him thrown into jail for not paying child support. To evade her, he hid when he came to town to see Cassidy, his wife at the time. Pat was very protective of Dad, and Dad trusted him. So he was the one that Dad kept in contact with. I understand now that I was just too young for Dad to put that kind of pressure on me.

Pat probably told you about our time with Dad at the Holiday Inn. Those times were really special to all of us. A few years later, Pat went into the military, and I lost touch with him until he was in Miami working at Ron Boucher's club, The Tom Jones Supper Club."

"I'm sure Pat told you about Ron. They were really close back then. Ron was the poorest kid in town when we were growing up. But he married Alice Bell, whose parents owned a packaging company. Alice's parents had a chauffeur drive her to school in a limousine daily! Talk about opposites attracting. The poorest kid in town married the heiress with a 22-million-dollar fortune. And that was 22 million dollars in 1970's money!"

Mike pauses and chuckles before continuing, *"When I turned 18, Pat asked me if I wanted to work with him at the club. It was 1973, and they changed the legal drinking age from 21 to 18 on July 1st. I turned 18 on July 2nd! So I would sit at the bar drinking and carrying on.*

Then there were the girls! Tom Jones Club was a cabaret. There were always beautiful dancing girls around. They had different events they used to draw customers. One time they announced, "Wednesday night, the girls will model lingerie if you want to buy something for your wife." Five or six girls would be naked in the back of the club, changing into lingerie. Oh, that was very exciting for an 18-year-old boy! I thought I was in heaven.

Of course, Ron Boucher was a character. I have plenty of stories about Ron and his escapades. For example, one night, I was out with Ron, shooting pool with some mob guys until around three a.m. Ron lost five grand to a pool shark, so I drove him back to the club to get the cash from the safe. But he was drunker than a skunk and couldn't open the safe! Pat had to meet us there to ensure no funny business went down. After all, I was eighteen years old and probably weighed 122 pounds soaking wet. That was the kind of absurd shit that went down.

I spent real time with my brother for the first time, and we had mutual respect. I was not his equal, but I think he saw me as more than just the younger brother. I also got to know a bit of a different side of Patrick than I had back in Indiana.

Of course, I'd heard the stories of Pat going out, getting in trouble, and being sent to the detention center. I listened to the rumors of him escaping in his bare feet. But I was the younger brother. I wasn't the one he would share all of that with. He probably figured I was hanging out with Mom and our two younger sisters at home."

Mike stops talking, laughs as he thinks about that, and continues, *"It was a fun summer for me. When I returned to Indiana in September, I took stock of my life and realized I did not want to spend the rest of it working in a factory. I was interested in video production. So I decided to join the Marine Corps. It was my way out of the cycle of poverty and dysfunction that we grew up in.*

In October of that year, I headed off to boot camp. While in the Corp, I didn't see much of Pat for a few years. But I did go with my Dad to see Pat and catch a Red Foxx show.

This was before Sanford and Sons, so he was still in the early stages of fame. Ron sent Pat, a 22-year-old kid, to collect the money for the mob. I only saw him once, so I don't know much about it. But I could tell he was packing a pretty hefty gun.

Patrick stayed in Miami for a few years, but I think he was tired of riding Ron's coattails and that whole lifestyle. One thing about Ron was that everything revolved around him when you were with him. Pat has always been his own person, so I can see how that would wear on him quickly. From what I know, he went to college for a bit and then headed out to LA."

"I followed my dream and learned video production in the Marine Corps. I talked my commanding officer into trading my gun for a camera.

I was stationed in California when he moved there, but I didn't see much of him. His son's mom, Connie, worked at Victoria Station Steakhouse. My sisters and I went to see him there once, I think.

I lived in California for thirty years! But Pat only stayed for a few years. He and Connie moved to New Mexico about the time Gabriel was born.

Once I left the Marines and finished college, I needed to find a job at a television station. Patrick said, "Why don't you come out to New Mexico? We can hang out…blah, blah, blah." You know the drill. Not having anything else lined up, I headed out to New Mexico to find work with my brother.

Pat was working at Jack's Lounge when I arrived. Jack's is where things started getting real interesting.

One night Pat said, "Hey, come out back." Now up until then, I had never done hard drugs. I'd smoked pot, done mushrooms, and what have you, but never the hard stuff. In the Marines Corps, guys were shooting up heroin and doing speed, but I didn't want anything to do with all of that.

I followed Pat to his car behind the bar and climbed in. He takes a little envelope and says, "I want you to taste this for me." "Sure," I confidently said, even though I had never even seen cocaine before that night. "Can you taste it and tell me if it's any good?" I must have had some idea of what to do with the cocaine because I tasted it and told him, "Oh yeah, I'm getting a sensation," like I knew what I was talking about!

That night I had no idea Patrick was getting ready to start dealing. Over the next few years, it went from a gram or two to ounces and finally to pounds. He went from making a couple hundred extra bucks to ten thousand, then to fifty thousand dollars, and it only went up from there. He was living the party life; by extension, so was I.

But Pat was always cautious. He kept everything quiet except for the couple of dozen people he sold to directly. I never saw him get drunk and out of control. He was never hooting and hollering or looking for a fight; none of that. He handled everything very discreetly.

We hung out at a bar called Ned's because it was open until 2 am. Once they closed for the night, we weren't locked out like ordinary customers. We would stay until about 5 am, doing this and that. He sold a lot of product there. We had "our table" in the bar's back corner, where we would sit every night. The bartender, Tracy, would hear that a customer was looking to score, and then it would happen. Years later, I found out Tracy was Olivia's first husband. I don't know why, but I never put it together back then.

My brother and I are both tall guys, Pat is a couple of inches taller and has broader shoulders, but I could hold my own. Pat knew everyone, and everyone liked him. He had good drugs, and the money was very good. But occasionally, some guy would come in looking for trouble.

One night as we walked across the bar, a couple of guys stood up and tried to square off against us. Pat and I can have mean faces. Those guys looked at us, turned around, and walked out. That's when I realized, "I'm safe. No one will mess with us when we're together."

"Of course, Pat had a rough side. He had to in that business, but he'd always had a bit of a temper. There is one incident that sticks out in my mind the most.

Pat's customers weren't your typical street junkies. He had a more high-class clientele, if you will. He used to deal coke to one of the heirs of the Wrigley gum fortune. Every month they got a substantial check from their trust. So it was normal for them to call and say, "Hey, we don't get our check until next week. We can't pay you now but will when the check comes in." Pat always fronted their cocaine, and they would pay up when they had the money. I have no idea how many thousands of dollars they would be in to Patrick for before they paid up.

They got strung up and were behind a couple of payments. Patrick had been calling, and they were ghosting him. Finally, he sent another guy and me over to collect. They still weren't paying up, so Patrick decided to come over to make his point in person.

He got to their house and demanded his money. Instead of giving it to him, they started making up bullshit stories and arguing with Pat. Well, he wasn't going to stand for that.

This was the late '70s. They had one of those open floor plan houses where the kitchen was open to the sunken living room a few steps below, which was popular then.

The more they talked, the angrier Pat got. I was only 21 years old and tried to be ready because things were tense, but I didn't know what to expect. I was in way over my head.

Pat was standing in the kitchen. Suddenly, without any warning, he twisted around, grabbed their massive, double-wide refrigerator, turned back around, and threw the entire fridge into the sunken living room below him! It crashed through their glass coffee table, which exploded, throwing glass everywhere! That's when I was like, "Woah, this is going to get serious!"

He made his point because they backed up, apologized, and paid the damn bill. Then they left town! We never heard from them again. To this day, I can't figure out how the hell he threw that huge refrigerator the way he did. Pat is not someone you want to piss off, especially not back then." Mike gives half a chuckle and pauses before continuing.

We ran a video production company for a while. We met some cool people and did some crazy things, like filming a crew looking for gold in the mountains. But eventually, Pat shut down the video production company and got into providing concert venues. Frank Tapia (a good friend of Patrick's) proposed buying a stage because the venue competition was low. Only one other guy was doing it.

We started getting all the big acts because the other owner charged over six grand for the bands to rent his stages.

As you can imagine, Pat's chosen profession worked well with the rock and roll lifestyle. They went together like peanut butter and jelly. So we had the drug angle covered too. While the union guys were building the stage, Pat and I took care of the tour managers' product needs in the back room.

It was the whole sex, drugs, and rock-and-roll party scene with the biggest bands of the day. But it was also a lot of work.

We would be at an arena with 18-20 doors where we had to set up turnstiles before the event. We did this a lot. After the turnstiles were ready, we would wait until it was time and then open all the doors simultaneously. Then 15,000 to 20,000 excited people would start to rush in!

I remember we'd set up all the turnstiles and waited for the countdown to open the doors. Five minutes before go time; three minutes, two minutes, "Everybody ready?" "Yes!" "You ready down there?" "Yes!" "Alright, standby!" Then we flung open the doors to the 20,000 excited fans. That's when we realized the turnstiles were all in backward. Every. Single. One. *"Holy shit! Turn the Turnstiles!' Turn them!" I was trying to yell over the sound of the fans pushing to get in. So there we were, rushing and trying to turn around all the damn turnstiles so we could get the people in!"* Mike stopped to catch his breath because he was laughing so hard.

"It wasn't too long after I moved to Albuquerque that I landed a job at a local television station in California. So I would fly back and forth between Cali and New Mexico for all these adventures." Mike continued.

"One day, Pat rang me up and asked, "Hey, do you want to go to Vegas this weekend?" I tell him, "Man, I can't afford that." He says, "Don't worry about it."

"So we go up to the TWA counter, and Pat says, "Do you have anything flying to Vegas in the next hour or two?" The lady behind the counter looks at us like scum under her feet and says, "It's sold out. There are only first-class tickets left." Pat shrugs, pulls a wad of cash out of his pocket, and says, "Yeah, okay. Give us two tickets." So we hop on the plane, and away we go.

Once we arrived at the casino, we headed to the enormous penthouse suite. Pat then opens his camera bag, takes out a tennis ball container, unscrews the bottom, and three or four grams of cocaine and forty thousand dollars in cash fall onto the bed. He shrugs and says, "Let's go have some fun!" So I took a bullet of coke, went down to the casino floor, and sat at the roulette table, sniffing coke and playing roulette.

We were there for three or four days and had a blast. Stupid, stupid stuff."

Recreating Patrick

"My journey getting clean was a lot different than Patrick's. First, I don't think I got into the drugs as deeply as he did. My wake-up call came on a plane ride back to California after an intense week of videography for an artist in Texas. I realized I was jonesing really bad. So I got up, went to the little bathroom on the plane, snorted some coke, and returned to my seat. After I sat down, I realized that this was not the life that I wanted. My television career was taking off. So I sold or snorted what I had brought back to California. But from that time on, cocaine lost its importance to me. I focused on moving up in my career."

"After that, Pat and I drifted apart for a while. Honestly, all of us siblings did during that time. We came back together as young adults when our Dad passed away. We returned to Indiana for the funeral. The people we grew up with asked us what we were doing for careers, etcetera. You know, the normal catching-up conversations. More than once, we heard, "Wow, you guys live some exciting lives. We grew up, exited Indiana, and headed out on our own adventures. Of course, there were some rough rides here or there, like with Patrick, but we did very well, considering how we grew up.

Unfortunately, it wasn't like that for our two younger sisters. We left home when they were still pretty young. So, they were there with Mom by themselves during some hard years. Mom was on and off welfare, getting sober, and stuff. I think they resented us older ones for leaving."

"Lora brought them to California for the summers. She'd get them jobs, but things would always fall apart, and they would end up back in Indiana. It was like they were stuck in a rut." Mike sighs. The guilt and pain are evident and still raw as he talks about his little sisters.

"All us older kids tried to help them out occasionally. But they always landed back in Indiana, where there were no jobs. Once Mom got sober, she took off and left them to fend for themselves. They got caught up in the cycle of poverty, welfare, having kids, and bouncing from marriage to marriage. All four of us had a lot of survivor's guilt about leaving our younger sisters with Mom. But we try to remember that we were kids, pulling ourselves up by our bootstraps. We could only do what we could do." The sadness of not getting them out of that life still weighs heavily on him.

"One of our younger sisters passed away seven years ago. She had come into a bit of money and tried to recreate what Dad used to do for us at the Holiday Inn. She rented a room and had a little party. Someone brought something to that party that was no good for her. She died of an overdose. It was hard."

"We also lost our oldest sister, Mary, to cancer a couple of years ago. She fought a long and hard battle against it, but eventually, it got her. Losing Mary unquestionably cut deep."

Our conversation lasted a few more moments as we talked about everyday things. He has a thriving videography business; much of his work is for online content these days. I can tell he has come to a place where he is content and fulfilled. Mike looks back on the past with wry humor and poignant insight. I am grateful for the nuanced view of Patrick's life, particularly the years he dealt drugs.

CHAPTER NINE

Drugs and Thugs

"The trouble with being smart is you know what happens next."

- Patrick Harrington

In 1976, I moved to Santa Fe, New Mexico wanting to make a go of the whole family thing with my son, Gabriel, and his mom, Connie. But I was too full of piss and vinegar to be a family man then. I drank more than ever, was running drugs, and had a wandering eye when it came to the ladies. The secrets still clawed up from my belly into my throat, strangling me any time I was sober enough to hear them. It didn't take long for the relationship with Connie to fall apart.

When we first arrived in New Mexico, I got a job managing two bars in the same building, one upstairs and the other down. It was a quiet biker bar. No one was looking for trouble. During the *Zozobra Festival*, *Burning Man* before *Burning Man* existed, we would have tourists come in, but the bars stayed peaceful even then.

Zozobra was created by Will Shuster and is celebrated yearly in Santa Fe. Will was a member of a group of artists that moved to Santa Fe in the 1920s. The first *Zozobra* was observed in his backyard when he burned a creepy six-foot-tall marionette he'd made. From those humble beginnings, the *Zozobra* festival grew into one of the largest yearly festivals in the country. The puppet has grown to be fifty feet tall! At the end of the festival, it is set aflame, signifying the burning away of the previous year's stress and pain.

When Connie and I split up, I got a job as a bartender at Jack's Lounge in Albuquerque. It was here that I met my good friend Frankie. He was a short, stocky Mexican guy and was damn witty. He had been a Green Beret in Vietnam and tough as hell. I loved him like a brother.

Frankie and I got this tiny apartment together. We had one chair, a small black and white TV, and I had a mattress. Eventually, Frankie got a mattress, too, then we were real high class! We also shared this fantastic little car that wouldn't start unless we pushed it down a hill until the engine caught. Eventually, we got some furniture and started dealing drugs out of that place.

Frankie, yeah, he was there from the very beginning in New Mexico, before all the drugs. Eventually, I would marry his cousin Rosanne. Frankie and I had some crazy times together. I miss him even though he passed some time ago.

Jack's Lounge could be a rough place. I've always had a sixth sense for when the crap is about to hit the fan. I could look at a guy and know he would be a problem. I kept browning behind the bar with me, but my fists usually did the trick. When things started to get ugly, I'd beat the tar out of the troublemakers and throw them out. To be honest, I enjoyed a good fight.

They called me *The Storm because I fought fast and hard. Using my fists allowed me to pound out the rage that consumed me despite my attempts to drown it in whiskey.*

People often threatened to call the cops on me for knocking the tar out of them. But they never did. They didn't want to deal with the cops any more than I did.

Around this time, my brother Mike left the Marines and finished his Videography degree. He didn't have a job, so I told him to come to New Mexico to do something together. He came out and became a part of the rock and roll and drug life I was about to begin.

I was tired of living paycheck to paycheck. And I still had this drive to be important and matter. I was not going to live my life in poverty as my parents had. I wanted money and would find a way to get that money come hell or high water. My mother used to say, *"Patrick is going to find a way to get what he wants, one way or another."*

I remember the day I went into the cocaine business like yesterday. I had $600 from my GI bill. The going rate for cocaine at the time was $2,400 an ounce. I took my $600 and bought a quarter ounce of cocaine.

I went straight home to my apartment. My brother was sitting at the kitchen table. I took the cocaine out of my pocket and threw it on the table in front of him. I looked at the cocaine, a sense of finality settling into the pit of my stomach. *"I hate this shit. I know where it is going to lead. But I guess we're going there."* I told him. And that was it. I was in the cocaine business. That quarter ounce soon became an ounce, then several ounces. Before long, I was selling kilos of coke.

Tricks of the Trade

The selling of cocaine was nothing; it was easy. What was hard was not getting caught. But being smart enough to outwit the law and not get busted was its own high! I had all kinds of tricks up my sleeves to keep the law off my back. I had different cars, safe houses where I would crash, and many stash houses around the city. I kept a stash in a couple lockers at the racquetball club, the pool hall, and all over the city, really. Hell, one time, I got coke straight out of the police evidence room!

I think what kept me the safest was that I trusted no one. I kept a low profile and lived my life in the shadows. Those who did know who

I was, knew better than to talk about me. I took my secrecy very seriously.

I always had high-grade product; some was even pharmaceutical grade. In fact, there were times I was told that it was so pure that I should hold onto it for myself and not sell it. *"If you start giving them (the customers) this, they will never be happy with normal stuff."*

I used to cut my product with baby laxatives. The laxatives came in blocks that we would crush into an extremely fine powder and mix with the cocaine.

I ran all over town, buying out any baby laxatives that I could find. Most of the time, I would send other people so I wouldn't look suspicious. I didn't want people to ask, *"What is this guy doing with all this baby laxative?"* One time I managed to buy a kilo block of baby laxative wholesale! You probably have never seen a kilo of laxatives. But let me tell you, that is a hell of a lot. But it wasn't long before it ran out, and we were back to buying out all the baby laxatives in Albuquerque.

I dated a hairdresser named Pam for a while. She was funny and quick-witted, and we had a good time together.

One day I dropped one of my cars off to be detailed. I had only dropped it off a few minutes before getting a call from the shop.

"Mr. Harrington, we need you to return to the shop at your earliest convenience."

"Why do you need me to come back? I only just dropped it off."

The voice on the other end got flustered, *"Um, well, sir, we found a large package of white powder in your trunk."* Now Pam, the witty girl she was, thought fast on her feet. She quickly chimed in loud enough for the shop guys to hear, *"Oh, that's mine. It's the chemicals that I use when dying people's hair. I must have forgotten to get it out of the trunk."* I don't remember if it was the actual cocaine or the cut! It was a close call either way. But man, once we took care of it, the whole situation was funny as hell.

A Big Man Living in the Shadows

Though my drug-dealing career started purely for financial reasons, it didn't take long before it became tangled with my pride and ego. The bigger I became in the drug world, the more "power" I had. I was the person everyone wanted to know. I was bullet proof.

I wasn't a back alley dealer. I only dealt with the social elite: politicians, lawyers, judges, and rock stars. Of course, it was all bullshit. People didn't care about me; they wanted the cocaine. But at the time, I felt like a big man, one of Satan's little tricks to keep me trapped. I'm not going to lie; there were some fun times, especially in the beginning. I had more money than I had ever imagined possible. Between the drugs and money came the girls, parties, and fame.

Every night I would blow through at least an ounce of good-quality cocaine. That was $2500 back then, and that was just the coke. It didn't include all the drinking and carousing. I would only snort cocaine using a $100 bill. What a wasteful way to live.

Yeah, I had money, but I suffered from *Elvis Pressley Syndrome.* I felt like I had to spend my money as fast as I got it; otherwise, someone would take it. This is how Satan kept me trapped. He made it hard to walk away even though the lifestyle was killing my body and my soul.

Although I had power and respect, I was always cautious. I kept a low profile and preferred to do things in the shadows through intermediaries. In fact, if someone came up to me and knew my name, I wanted to know how they had found out who I was.

Besides my stash houses and cars all over the city, I never drove the same route twice in a row. I trusted no one and was always on high alert. I was like a chameleon, blending in with the background wherever I went. I didn't wear a vest with a patch on it that announced to the world, *"Hey, I'm into all kinds of criminal crap."* I wore leather jackets, gold chains, and cool boots, which is a profile in itself when you think about it.

It was an exhausting way to live, but it is why I didn't end up dead or with an extended stay in federal prison. Most people I knew from that time are either dead from a bullet to the head or an overdose. The ones that didn't die spent most of their lives behind steel bars. After all the glitz, glamor, and parties, this is how life in the drug business ends. Behind the façade is a life of loneliness, paranoia, addiction, violence, and, ultimately, death. I am blessed to have made it out alive, but only God could restore my sanity.

My brother, Frankie, and I all had experience in one aspect of video production or another. So when I came across the opportunity to buy the first portable, professional Sony video camera on the market, I jumped. I bought it from a Sony rep for less money than it was worth. The camera recorded to beta tape and had this big battery pack that someone had to tote around. The whole kit was huge, clunky, and heavy, but it was top-of-the-line stuff back then.

We took that camera and our combined knowledge and started a video production company named *No cover, No Minimum.* Our specialty was demo reels for local bands, including *The Planets.*, an up-and-coming act being courted by major recording studios. We met them at *Ned's* (the bar where I hung out and did business).

We agreed to record one of their concerts and handle the security and venue. We rented a local biker roadhouse bar. They had beer, liquor, and a big dance hall to stage the concert, all essentials for a successful rock concert! We hired the local chapter of the *Banditos* to run the floor and handle security (I'm not sure where we came up with that *brilliant* idea).

To cover expenses, we charged a cover charge to get into the concert. The *Banditos* worked the door, collecting the cover charge before letting anyone inside. Before long, the roadhouse was filling up, and the party was getting rolling. I was standing in the back, organizing everything from the shadows, where I was most comfortable.

After an hour or so, one of my guys told me that the *Bandito*s working the door weren't charging their *Outlaw* (another biker gang) and *Bandito* friends to get in. I found the Road Captain and said, *"Look, we have to make money to pay you. Your guys can't be letting their friends in for free."* He shut that crap down real fast; they wanted to get paid too. They didn't let in any more freeloaders after that. In the biker gang world, once an order is issued from the guy in charge, that's it. You don't buck the hierarchy because the consequences are harsh and sometimes deadly.

The alcohol was flowing, and the music was rocking, but it wasn't long before some locals started getting out of hand. I started towards the commotion to handle it, but when I got closer, I saw the guy on the floor. *"What happened?"* I asked one of the guys working for me. *"He was getting out of line, so one of the Banditos knocked him out."* One thing was for sure when they handled a situation it was handled once and for all! I nodded to the guy on the floor and said, *"Get him out of here!"* The show continued without a pause.

A little later, Mike yells in my ear, *"Three people are climbing through the back window with a video camera."* We couldn't have that. First, they needed to pay the cover charge to see the show. Secondly, we were recording the concert professionally. We didn't want people making their own bootleg concert recordings. *"I'll handle it,"* I told Mike, already walking to the back. *"Do you have your gun?"* Mike asked. *"I always have a gun,"* I pointedly looked around the room, *"But I only have so many bullets. So I think I'll try another tactic first."*

"This is a private event. You'll have to go to the front door and pay the cover charge, just like everyone else. Also, you'll have to leave the camera in your car because a professional production team is filming the concert." I tell the two men and woman standing by the back window.

"Hey, no problem. But can I talk to you?" asked the guy with a long beard. He looked like one of the bikers we had handling security.

"Sure," I said.

"We're in the area playing a show with another band. We heard *The Planets* were playing tonight. We just wanted to get a look at them. We've heard good things," he explained.

"Yeah, cool. What band are you with?" I asked.

He kind of chuckled. *"We're part of ZZ top. As a matter of fact, I AM ZZ Top."* This was before MTV and all of that. If I knew what I do now, man. I had their very first video! I have no idea what happened to that film. Maybe I'll find it packed away one of these days.

"Let me buy you a drink." He said.

So I sat at the bar, drinking and shooting the breeze with Billy Gibbons until all hell broke loose at the concert again, and I had to deal with it.

Later I walked them out to their car. Man, did he have a sweet ride! It was a 1965 Cadillac Eldorado Biarritz with hydraulics, so it would jump and all that crazy stuff. A cool guy with a cool car!

I caught one of their shows while on the road with SkyHawk Rugs a few years ago. Don't worry; I used the front door.

We attended a Rolling Stones concert in New Orleans a few months later because I was their drug hook-up.

I didn't even use the stuff when I first started selling. But when I did start using it, I hid it from everyone. If people found out I was using, everyone would want to do a bump with me, and I would end up even more screwed up than I already was. But I couldn't hide it forever. People found out my secret at the Stones concert.

I didn't make it difficult to figure out when I kept disappearing into the bathroom and returning with a raging case of the sniffles. The crowd I hung with certainly knew what that meant. This was a turning point for me. I began to use more coke and lose more of the control I thought I had over my addictions.

Our video production company was getting noticed and offered more jobs. This dovetailed nicely into my more lucrative, full-time career as a cocaine distributor.

The Lost Dutchman's Mine

One of my cocaine clients asked if we would be interested in filming an expedition to search for the Lost Dutchman's Mine in Arizona's Superstition Mountains.

According to legend, a prospector named Jacob Waltz, referred to as *"the Dutchman,"* hit a vein of incredibly high-grade gold but died before he could mine it out. He dictated a map to a neighbor before dying in 1891.

However, neither the neighbor nor the thousands of treasure hunters who have come since have ever found the mine. Whether the gold mine exists is open to debate, but they definitely found a box of high-grade ore under his bed after he died.

A picture of the box is at The Superstition Mountain Museum located in Apache Junction. Also in the museum are carved stones with maps and clues to find the mine. I received special permission to photograph these stones before going on the expedition. I still have slides of the images packed away somewhere. The museum also has a memorial to all the people who have lost their lives in the mountains.

Expeditions to look for the mine are dangerous. Other treasure hunters and mine operators won't hesitate to take shots at people who trespass or are close to finding the mine. Also, the Superstition Mountains are incredibly rugged, with extreme temperature fluctuations. Pocketed with box canyons, steep drop-offs, and ledges, the mountains pose a significant danger to hikers and adventurers.

We were excited to join the expedition. The team we partnered with had the permits to dig and explore the area where they believed the Dutchman's Lost Mine to be.

I arrived at base camp wearing my new, rugged Redwing boots. It looked like a military camp, with large tents, a common outdoor area, and armed men milling around. I was already well-armed, but they issued my brother, Mike, a gun. They told us that no one was to leave camp unarmed. They were sure that claim jumpers watched them, waiting for their chance to take the mine.

Every morning we would trek out, carrying the camera. I would tote the backpack with the beta tape machine and the battery. The pack was connected to the camera by double cords about ten feet long. It was quite the workout carrying that heavy pack up and down the mountains all day!

Of course, I supplied them with cocaine, so we all got to be pretty close. Frankie, Mike, me, and some other guys started bringing our girlfriends to the mountains on our motorcycles. We'd all live in tents while filming and party at night. It was a good time, sitting in one of the most beautiful places on earth, talking about lost treasure, and getting high.

On one of these trips into the mountains with our girls, the cops pulled us over for speeding. I had my gun and cocaine on me; I just knew this was it for me! I was heading to prison. Quickly, I slipped the gun and coke to my girlfriend before the cop got to us, a kind of "Hail Mary" move. The cop searched my bike and me but never searched my girlfriend! Another close call that I walked away from unscathed.

In April, the expedition ended when the heat made it too dangerous to continue. They never found The Dutchman's Lost Mine, but we sure did have a great time looking for it!

Sometime later, another group approached us, claiming they had research that proved Dutchman's mine was in Texas. They even had a handmade gold bar that they said proved their claim. They asked us to come to film the expedition, which we did.

We followed a ranger up into the Teja Mountains and filmed the journey. Unfortunately, this whole experience was a shit show. They sued us for the rights to the film we made. The court case dragged on for years. In the end, we had to give them some of the footage. The whole experience soured me on the entire business. It was time to do something new. So I bought a rock and roll stage.

Drugs and Rock and Roll

I know this won't shock most of you, but more than a few drug deals go down at rock concerts. I would work security for the big acts that came through Albuquerque. This allowed me to sell to the people I needed to without drawing attention to myself; I was ever the chameleon.

My friend Frankie came to me one day with an idea to make the concert angle more lucrative. *"Albuquerque is on the tour bus routes for all the big concert tours. They love stopping here because it is almost all profit for them. It doesn't take them out of their way at all. But only one guy owns the stages here in town, and he charges an arm and a leg."* I don't know what you know about building stages, but they are simple, just lumber and scaffolding for the most part. The only overhead is the labor because you have to work with the union. It was a no-brainer, really. We bought the stage, we provided the security for the shows, and I was able to deal cocaine to the band promoters, managers, etc., without being conspicuous.

We got really involved in the whole scene. We partied hard with the bands, promoters, roadies, and groupies. It was the cool, glamorous world of sex, drugs, and rock and roll. It was all bullshit. Even in all of this, I hung back in the shadows. I was the guy, the legend; I got off on being the mysterious guy in the background that had the power.

My drug name was *The Breeze* because I was like a cool breeze. Like the wind, I was invisible and would slip through your fingers.

In 1980 Reagan was elected President, and Nancy Reagan made her platform *"Just say no to drugs!"* This was ironic because the biggest importer of cocaine in the US at the time was the CIA.

The Contras were various right-wing rebel groups funded by the CIA to oppose and overthrow the Marxist Nicaraguan government. The Contras used the money from their drug trafficking to pay for their war on the Nicaraguan government. The CIA would traffick the drugs into LA to help their war efforts.

I have a close friend that trafficked drugs for the CIA at the time. I didn't get involved in all of that. Though, I'm sure I handled and sold the cocaine they had trafficked.

On the one hand, the CIA was flooding the streets of LA with cocaine; on the other hand, the First Lady was leading the charge against drugs. I am sure the CIA shielded Reagan and Nancy from knowing the truth, but it was a weird time to be in the drug business.

Once the *"Just Say No to Drugs"* campaign started, the DEA monitored the concert scene more closely. I only ever watched the concerts from backstage, but now, because of the increased scrutiny, I didn't go at all. I sent someone else to handle the drug deals for me. I was already a careful SOB, but now I was flat-out paranoid. I never let anyone take my picture. I freaked out if a new person knew my name. I constantly looked over my shoulder, doubling back, never taking the same route twice. But is it paranoia if someone actually is out to get you?

Vegas, Baby!

When I needed to relax and get away, I would hop on a plane and head to Sin City. There I could ride the endless roulette wheel of partying, drugs, and sex without the pressure of being the guy in charge.

I would use my camera bag or a tennis ball tube to smuggle cocaine and forty or fifty thousand dollars onto the plane.

I remember one trip, a swarm of feds met the plane. Again, I thought, "This is it! They finally caught me." I ditched the camera bag on the plane and filed off with the other passengers. I  was shocked. I just walked past the feds and out of the airport. The next day I got a call from the airline asking me to return to the airport and go to their customer service counter. I debated whether or not to show up, worried that the feds might have set a trap. Ultimately, I decided that not showing up would be more suspicious.

I walked up to the airline counter, looking cool and calm as a cucumber, but I was sweating bullets on the inside. The guy at the counter asked for my ID. Once I had shown it, he handed me back my camera case. *"Dude, there is a wad of cash in there. I didn't want you to lose it!"*

"Yeah, I forgot this in the chaos of disembarking the plane yesterday. Thanks for holding it for me." I nonchalantly replied, as if leaving the case had been an accident.

"I would have been freaked to lose that kind of money." He said.

I made a little more small talk, thanked him again, and casually walked out of the airport for the second time in two days. This time I was carrying fifty thousand dollars and the still hidden cocaine.

On one trip, I invited my brother Mike to come along. As was my practice, I just walked up to the airline counter and asked for tickets on the next plane to Vegas. The airline agent looked me up and down and snootily told me that there were no seats available on the flight except two in first class. It was clear that she didn't expect these two sketchy-looking young guys to be able to afford first class. I just shrugged and said, *"We'll take them."* Then I handed her the cash like it was nothing because it was nothing to me back then. Let me tell you, that set her back on her heels a bit.

When we landed, I brought Mike to the suite I had booked. Then I dumped out my camera bag and handed him a wad of cash and some coke. We flew high that weekend, partying nonstop. I did this kind of spur-of-the-moment crap all the time. As long as I kept the party going, I didn't have to face the demons always in the background of my mind waiting to attack my sanity.

CHAPTER TEN

The Descent

"I don't give the Devil his due. But there is a devil out there. I've seen it. I've lived it."

- Patrick Harrington

It would be easy to think that I was living the high life. I had more money than I knew how to spend. I was surrounded by people who called themselves my friends and was invited to all the best parties with the coolest people. The boy who always looked for acceptance and to be needed was now one of the most powerful drug traffickers in New Mexico.

But instead of feeling fulfilled, I grew more and more paranoid. Being in the drug business is not for the faint of heart. You have to watch your back because someone is always trying to take your business. The people you call friends are just using you for the drugs you can provide them. If that isn't enough, you are constantly dodging the law, covering your tracks, and then doing it all again. That is enough to make anyone paranoid. As they say, you aren't crazy if they are out to get you.

To succeed and survive in the drug business, you must do things that scar your soul, things ordinary people would never even consider doing. You become hard-hearted and cold.

Drugs and friendships don't mix. When push comes to shove, my profession would always come before relationships.

I was a long-time dealer to a wealthy couple in Albuquerque. They had backed the expedition into the Superstitious Mountains to look for the Dutchman's Lost Mine. They hired our production company to do the videography. They hired us largely because we would provide quality video production, and I could also provide quality cocaine. It was a two-for-one win for them.

She was an heiress to a candy empire, and he was in the music business. They had a friend living with them that they vouched for. When someone vouches for someone else, I expect they will pay what they owe, and if they don't, you will cover their debt. Their friend was in debt to me for several thousand dollars worth of cocaine. I called and told them I expected payment for the coke. Instead of paying, they started dodging my calls. I had to leave town for business and told my brother Mike to handle the situation.

When I returned, Mike reported that their friend had skipped town and not paid. By this time, I was extremely pissed off. I called once more, demanding they tell me where their friend was. They tried to lie and say that they didn't know. But I knew that they had gone to visit him.

That was it. I was done. I told Joey and Mike to strap up, and we headed to their mansion. I burst into their house, demanding they either pay me or tell me where their buddy was.

Now Joey was a rough guy having connections with the New York mob. He started working this wealthy couple over real good because that's how he did things, but I still wasn't getting the answers I needed.

I've always been a big guy and was pretty strong when I was young. The anger I felt for being betrayed and lied to roiled within me. I was high on cocaine and adrenaline as I stood in their kitchen, yelling for them to give me my money. Something snapped inside me. I spun around, picked up their huge, professional-grade refrigerator, and threw it across the room. It landed in the sunken living room a few steps down from us. After that, they paid up quick. Then we took their Mercedes and left. They never complained or said a word. I was told they packed up and left town two days later, and I never heard from them again.

But what I remember the most from that day is after I threw the refrigerator, I saw their young daughter staring at me and crying. I never even considered that their kids might be home, and though it shames me now to admit it, even if I had known, I don't think I would have done anything differently. When you deal drugs, your reputation protects you more than anything else. If it got around that I had allowed someone to steal from me and I didn't do anything about it, others would think they could get away with stealing or even more. This is just what it is to be in the drug business.

The business and the drugs took a toll on all areas of my life. I have many regrets from those years. I was a hard man; I didn't allow anyone to cross me. That was true for the people I did business with and the women I dated.

The Julies

I once dated a woman named Julie. Actually, I dated two women named Julie, and they were both batshit crazy. To keep them straight, I'll call them Julie One and Julie Two.

Julie One and I would have knockdown, drag-out fights all the time. Two drug addicts cannot have a healthy relationship because drugs will always be the most important thing in their lives. We were having one of our fights when Julie One grabbed a bank bag with forty-five grand in cash that I had for emergencies. She ran out the door and down the street, higher than the empire state building, screaming at the top of her lungs. *"You know the man that lives in that house? He's a drug dealer!"* I chased her down, dragged her back to the house, beat some sense into her, and took back the bank bag.

She left me and moved back home with her mom. About a week later, out of my mind, drunk and high, I went to her mom's house to talk. But she refused to see me. So I drove my car through their garage door!

I should have been arrested and dealt with some serious legal fallout. But, I dealt coke to one of the best lawyers in town, and he got me a sweet deal. In the end, I just had to pay their insurance bill and a fine to the court. But my relationship with Julie One was over.

I took my son, Gabriel, and Julie Two to Disney Land for a vacation. I loved giving my son all the things I never had growing up. We spent the first few days riding all the rides and having a great time. After dinner, we would return to the hotel and party at the hotel bar while Gabriel was alone and asleep in the hotel room.

One night, I was exhausted and wanted to go back to our room. But Julie Two wasn't done partying. We argued for a few minutes, but she refused to budge; she was staying. Over all the drama, I left her at the bar and went to bed.

Julie Two never came back to the hotel room that night. Instead, she shacked up with some guy she met at the bar. I was pissed! I spent a small fortune bringing her to Disney Land, only for her to cheat on me with some other dude. When she returned to the room, we had a doozy of a fight, screaming at each other and throwing things. My son, Gabriel, was there watching us fight and carry on.

Julie Two spun away from me, grabbed my gun from the nightstand, and pointed it directly at me. Gabriel yelled, *"Don't you shoot my dad. If you kill him, I'm going to call the police!"*

She did pull the trigger. However, she didn't know that I'd unloaded the gun as a precaution because I had a feeling that something like that might happen. I grabbed the gun from her and beat her senseless while my son looked on. It was a messed up, ugly, shameful day that hurts to think about now. But it happened, and I can't undo it. One of my deepest regrets is that I continued the cycle of trauma with Gabriel.

After getting sober, I realized I would never have to put my hands on a woman's throat. I was raised thinking this was how a man should handle women. It was an amazing and freeing feeling to be rid of that mindset. From that day until now, I have never struck another woman. Thanks to God and sobriety, I am a better man.

Rock Bottom

By this time, I was spiraling fast toward rock bottom. I couldn't make it through the day without being high and drunk. Everywhere I looked, I saw people following me. I lived life in a state of complete paranoia.

I couldn't sleep. I covered all of my windows with aluminum foil so my house would be completely dark and no one could see in the windows. I would lock myself in my bedroom, surrounded by my guns, vodka, and Vicodin.

I had to drink a 20-ounce tumbler of vodka, snort half an ounce of coke, and take a few Vicodin to sleep. Even then, I would only sleep for two hours. Then I would wake up and do it all over again. Toward the end, I lived in a constant alcohol poisoning.

I would disappear, causing my friends to worry. After a few days, they would knock on my door, trying to check on me. But I never answered their calls or the door.

One of my friends would climb into the house through the doggy door in my kitchen. Everyone knew I slept with more guns than a battleship. So to avoid having his brains shot out, he would belly crawl through my house to my bedroom to ensure I was still alive. Later I would realize what a good friend he was, but, in those moments, I was just mad. I yelled that it wasn't any of his damn business if I was alive or dead. I was such a cold, hard bastard back then.

One night, I stopped by the pharmacy and bought two bottles of Nyquil on my way home. I drank my tumbler full of Vodka, snorted my coke, popped my Vicoden, and drank down both bottles of Nyquil. That turned out to be a really bad idea. I couldn't talk or move for two full days. I honestly thought that I was going to die. On top of everything else, the Nyquil threw me for a loop. I haven't touched Nyquil since that day!

I had chronic insomnia due to addictions and paranoia, so I was always desperate for sleep. I remember one night, the insomnia was horrible. It had been at least a week since I had slept at all. I drank my vodka, snorted my cocaine, and popped some Vicodin.

However, I freaked out because I was afraid I would die of an overdose. So I ran into my backyard and made myself vomit into the grass. Then I tried to sleep but instead stared at the damn ceiling, counting the ticking seconds. I scrounged around, looking for another Vicodin but couldn't find one. Desperate for relief from the insomnia, I went to the backyard and began to dig through my vomit, looking for the pills. You don't know the meaning of rock bottom until you are in your backyard scrounging through your own vomit for drugs.

These were the darkest times of my life. The pain and shame make it hard for me to go back there, but I need the memory because it helps keep me sober.

I made it through those dark days through God's grace and protection. I don't enjoy remembering those times. I'm ashamed of what I became. But the only way to understand the miracle of my sobriety is to understand just how low I got.

My drug associates were either dying or going to federal prison to do hard time. My mind was splintering from the combination of drugs, alcohol, trauma, and PTSD. One day, I decided I was done. It was time to get sober.

The Serenity Prayer

God grant me the serenity to accept the things I cannot change, the courage to change the things I can, and the wisdom to know the difference, living one day at a time; enjoying one moment at a time; taking this world as it is and not as I would have it; trusting that You will make all things right if I surrender to Your will.

CHAPTER ELEVEN

Journey to Sobriety

"The biggest amends I can make to society is that I don't do it again. And I haven't done it for 36 years and counting."

- Patrick Harrington

There are some dates that are sacred, dates that will forever be associated with something momentous. On December 7, 1941, Pearl Harbor was bombed. On July 4, 1776, the U.S. declared independence from Great Britain. On July 14, 1986, Patrick Harrington took his last drink and did his last drugs. This is my personal independence day, the first day of the rest of my life.

I remember the first Alcoholics Anonymous meeting that I attended. I was on edge, unsure who I would see and what they would say. I wore my cowboy hat and boots, which had become my armor against the world. I sat in the back of the room, stone-faced, and didn't say a word to anyone. I refused even to give them my name, paranoid that someone attending would know me and turn me in to the Feds or kill me. I continued to show up but did not begin to let my guard down for a long time.

I trusted no one. My entire life, I had figured I would die from a gunshot wound to the head. Sitting in the AA meetings, I still expected that bullet to be aimed my way. I was in such a dark, ugly, grim place. I can't explain it in a way anyone could understand unless they've lived it. If you are only as sick as your secrets, I was the equivalent of  the walking plague. My secrets had secrets, and they were slowly eating me alive.

After a few weeks, a man approached me and offered to sponsor me. Mike Eves, I knew him from the drug world. He was a big-time drug trafficker in New Mexico and the southwest United States. We moved in the same circles but never crossed paths before meeting at AA. Mike truly understood me and the life I was trying to escape in a way that no one else could. One day he said, *"Look, Patrick, it doesn't matter what you tell these people in the meeting. You can attend and never tell them a damn thing about yourself. Just keep coming and keep listening."*

When doing drugs or drinking, you never have to face your demons. You use your addiction to silence, ignore, and push them further into your soul. But when you begin to get sober, you suddenly have all these demons, feelings, and PTSD to handle. But you have no coping strategies to deal with anything because addiction was your panacea for managing anything life threw your way.

People who have never fought addiction tend to focus on the physical withdrawal symptoms, from getting the toxins out of your body to overcoming your brain's chemical dependence on them. But what is less understood are the psychological effects of getting sober.

Psychologically, getting sober felt like standing in a room with hundreds of people dressed as your worst nightmares and screaming at the top of their lungs for hours on end. You can't leave the room. You can't cover your ears. You just have to deal with them screaming in your face.

I had always struggled with insomnia but could force myself to sleep an hour or two by drinking and taking sedatives. Now my only method for falling asleep was gone. I went for days without sleeping at all. I tried everything I could to sleep: exercising, reading, and watching TV, but nothing worked. The exhaustion made me feel like I was slowly going insane. I was desperate for even a few hours of sleep. But it was proving as elusive as finding the Holy Grail.

Finally, I discovered going to the movies. I felt safe in the back corner of a dark theater. I would go to a matinee, and the film would put me to sleep for an hour or two. This was the only way for me to fall asleep for a long time.

For years my life had revolved around working, which was selling drugs and various business ventures that allowed me better access and ways to hide my drug business dealings. Now I had nothing to do. I do not tolerate boredom well. I still had plenty of money from my previous career, so I bought a couple of horses. At the time, I owned a ranch outside of Albuquerque. So horses made sense.

Horse Therapy

Up until this point, I had never ridden a horse in my life. I had to teach myself to ride and care for a horse. This gave me things to focus on beyond my own swirling thoughts. I often think that buying those horses saved my life. Now I had something else that depended on me, something I had to care for. They gave me a sense of purpose.

I would saddle up and ride through the mountains of New Mexico for days on end. Those rides helped me process my emotions and some of the crazy stuff that lived inside my head. During this time, I learned how healing nature and animals can be for those overcoming addiction or dealing with PTSD.

One afternoon, I was riding when something in the brush caught my eye. Curious, I rode over to see what it was. Tangled in the branches of a scrub brush was a beat-up teddy bear. Suddenly, in an instant, I was transported back to the orphanage. I remembered the little boy with the bed beside mine and our shared teddy bear.

I had pushed down all those memories for years. But in the remote New Mexican mountains, I remembered myself as a traumatized four-year-old. A boy who desperately needed to be important enough to keep around—the boy who had hated oatmeal. I thought about the boy who had made a friend that shared what little comfort they had. I wonder what happened to that other little boy. I don't remember his name, but I remember that teddy bear and his friendship.

I started drinking before I hit puberty. Taking drugs followed soon after. Getting sober after that many years of addiction was a momentous challenge. I could not do it alone. Besides AA, my horses, and my sponsor, I was in an intensive outpatient program for years.

Dogs and Falcons

After I had learned about horses, I met a man who flew falcons. He was also a recovering addict and had been in the drug business.

When he talked about the pure adrenalin rush of flying falcons, I knew I had to try it. When I told Mike Eves about my new pursuit, he got excited because he was a master falconer. He started as a kid but got out of it when he got sick.

He taught me all he knew, and I still wanted to learn more. There is nothing like removing that hood and seeing that majestic bird lift off and soar. Unlike horses, birds do not bond with you. They are independent and could take off and never come back. The only bond you can establish with a falcon is a food bond.

Flying falcons requires intense focus and discipline. When I started flying them, it was legal to trap them or even find a nest and hatch them. They are now endangered, so stealing eggs is highly illegal. You will land yourself in serious hot water if you try it.

Once you have your bird, you must teach them to depend on you and only you for food. You have to establish that bond. Eventually, you can hand-feed them strips of meat but don't be deceived; they are still wild and fierce predators.

It takes a lot of work; sometimes, you must spend hours beating the brush looking for your bird. But once you set your bird free and they return to you, wow! What a feeling!

They are majestic creatures to watch. Learning the discipline to fly birds was a huge step in my sobriety. It taught me self-discipline in other areas of my life.

After learning to train falcons, I started training dogs. The dogs go and retrieve the kill, but you have to keep them focused, and they give and require an emotional relationship. Whereas a falcon only has a food bond, dogs bond deeply with you emotionally. I had no idea how to make an emotional connection. From early on, that area of my growth had been stunted. Training dogs helped me grow and heal this part of my psyche. That emotional disconnection contributed to my addiction. Learning to connect was a big part of my sobriety journey.

Training horses, falcons, and dogs presented a different challenge and taught me something that helped my life and recovery. Horses cannot be muscled or forced to do anything. You have to think ahead of them. Falcons learn every mistake you teach them. So you must be careful and conscious of what you are teaching them. But you can't get impatient or angry with them because they will just fly away. Dogs are much easier to train but need companionship and attention.

Falconry is not just a hobby or a sport. It is a lifestyle. The falcons are intensive in their training. You have to feed, house, and care for each animal. It takes most of your time.

Through falconry and raising horses and dogs, I learned weather patterns, math, reading terrain, how to hunt, discipline, and more. Once trained, your horse, falcon, and dogs work together. They are puzzle pieces that create a whole.

So it was in my recovery and sobriety. God brought different puzzle pieces into my life to help me on my journey. Movies, horses, falcons, dogs, Mike Eves, and Olivia were each one of those puzzle pieces.

I once asked God why he left me out there for so long. He replied, "Because you absolutely insisted on it."

Corvettes and Sobriety

When I started getting sober, I also lost my way career. I was a damn good drug dealer, but now I was out of work and was in no physical or mental condition to work.

I still had a lot of money when I left the drug business. I paid for my treatment program, which cost me about $100,000 over the years I was there. I also lived on that money for a long time. But no matter how much money you have, it only lasts so long when you spend it and don't make more. After a while, my stash of cash began to dwindle.

A few years before I got sober, my buddy Ted (aka Sandman) was on a trip to Baltimore. Sandman was a great guy. He wasn't into the hard drug world like I was. However, he was an excellent pot grower and restored cars. While on his trip, he came across an old, broken-down '62 Corvette. He knew owning a '62 Corvette was one of my dreams. He called me and said, "Hey, I found a grey '62 Corvette. The front end needs to be rehung. It needs extensive bodywork, and I don't know how much  mechanical work it needs. But we could make this car beautiful!"

I thought a minute and asked him, "Does the clock work?"

"I don't know. Hang on a minute, and I'll go check."

A few short minutes later, he returned to the phone, "Yup, the clock works."

"Buy it," I told him without hesitation. I was finally getting my Corvette!

It took a couple of years, but we got that car purring like a kitten, and she was gorgeous. We painted her faun beige and completely redid the interior. By the time she was done, I was on my way to getting sober. I didn't drive her around a lot, but when I did, what a ride!

One day, I was driving the Corvette around town and loving life. Then out of nowhere, the cravings hit me hard. I drove straight to an AA meeting and talked through what I was feeling. Afterward, a lady in the meeting said she could tell I was shaken up. But to hang on. I still remember her words of encouragement. Remember, your words are important. You never know how they can help someone else. This was one of those pivotal days in my life. It was the first time the cravings hit hard, and I made it through sober! It wasn't pretty, but I made it. Remember, you don't get points for style. The only thing that matters is that you don't drink or use.

Another day while I was out driving, a man approached me while I was parked. He offered to buy the Corvette right then and there. It was my dream car, and I didn't want to let it go. But I hadn't worked in a while, and I had a mortgage to pay, a kid to take care of, and I still had to pay for my IOP. The man promised me he wasn't buying it to turn around and sell it. He said it was for his wife. I didn't buy that BS. I knew he was probably just looking for a way to make a profit. But I needed the cash. So I sold it.

Later, I told my sponsor, Mike Eves, how I felt. I remember him saying, "It's just for now. One day you can buy one again."

Years later, once my business was successful, I began seriously looking for another Corvette. I was in Florida to have Scott Kietzmann chop my Victory Hammer. He changed out the rear fender and put a big 300 wheel on. That bike was a thing of beauty. I rode it for years before selling it and buying a Victory Cross Country.

While I was getting sober, I stopped riding for a time. I knew it was too dangerous for me while I was depressed and anxious. I didn't want to repeat that night in Fort Knox, where I tried to kill myself while riding.

While in Florida, I found my Corvette, a brand new 2007 atomic orange thing of beauty. I walked into the dealership, wrote a check for the full price, and had her shipped across the country to Cody, Wyoming. She still sits in my garage, a testament that things you lose in the hard times can be restored again.

Olivia

I withdrew from everyone I knew other than my sponsor. Everyone I knew before was part of the drug world I had left. So I spent a lot of time by myself, thinking. This was a critical time in my sober journey. I would go to Olivia's restaurant, *The Blue Chip Café*, and spend hours eating and thinking at a table. She made a fantastic sandwich!

I had known Olivia's husband, Tracy, for years before he died. He was a bartender at *Ned's*, where I did much of my business. We were good friends. I even attended their wedding.

One of my best friends was Olivia's brother. He and I ran hard back in the day. He was a large part of my years as a trafficker. We got up to some pretty crazy shit, let me tell you!

Once I got sober and left that life, I had to cut all contact with him. I loved him but had to completely remove myself from the people who had been a part of that. Even after we got married, I stayed away from him. I think he probably needed the space between us for his sobriety journey too. It's only been in the last few years that we reconnected. We are both old men now. Those years are long gone, and rebuilding our friendship is wonderful.

But even though I knew her husband and was good friends with her brother, Olivia and I only knew each other in passing. She said I was extremely closed off the few times she met me. She wasn't comfortable around me back then, even though she knew nothing about me or what I did for a living. But now I was sober and spent a lot of time in her restaurant, so we would chat.

When I started hanging out there, I was married to my first wife, but our relationship was toxic. After I got sober, I thought getting married and settling down would be good. But I was in no way ready for a relationship, much less a marriage. Roseanne and I fought all the time. One day as we fought, I threw her purse against the wall and stormed out. I spent the night driving aimlessly and thinking about what I had done. I knew I did not want to be the man who threw things and yelled at his wife. The following day, I went home and told her it was over. I explained that I wanted to be a better man and she deserved to be treated better. We brought out the worst in each other, not the best. I left that day and swore to not yell or throw things in my next relationship. I was breaking the toxic cycles that I had seen growing up.

Through all this, I continued hanging out at Olivia's restaurant. We were both single. I divorced Rosanne, and Olivia divorced her first husband because of his drinking. He died not long after because of the booze. Over time, our chats grew into a relationship. I don't remember when we started "dating." It happened organically. I had been sober for around five years when she invited me to attend a play with her. We began to travel and do more things together. I had no idea we were dating until we were in a full-fledged relationship. I once asked her, "Could you have imagined us being together when we first met?" "God, no! You were unapproachable!"

Before Olivia, I had never seen, much less been in a healthy relationship. When we got together, she was already a whole person. I was also a whole person. We weren't looking for another person to fix us or fill some hole in our lives. Instead, we could be who we were and enjoy the other person for who they were.

I was shocked the first time Olivia called me to tell me she was on her way home. I didn't know how to respond. I wasn't used to a partner who did those little, kind things that make you feel special.

Another day, Olivia told me she was thinking about buying a truck. She had a long drive between our house and her job at the Bureau of Land Management in Albuquerque. She felt a truck would be safer for the commute that she had to make. I said, "No problem. I'll go with you to look at them." She smiled and said, "No, I have it taken care of. Thanks though." Then she went and bought herself a beautiful 4x4 truck. She didn't need me to pick it out or pay for it. She had everything covered on her own.

When my buddy heard that Olivia had bought her own truck, he said, "You let her do that?" I laughed and said, "I don't let Olivia do anything. She does what she wants and doesn't need me like that."

Finally, I asked her to move in with me. She thought about it and then said she had two conditions. First, I needed to redo the bedroom because it was too small. Second, "no animal heads on the wall." Well, I could handle those! So we redid the bedroom, and I gave my buddy the moose head I had mounted.

I never worried that Olivia would run around on me, cheat, and party. Olivia just didn't do that kind of thing. Instead, she was open and communicated with me. Instead of worrying about our relationship, I could focus on the man I was meant to be and grow my business.

I know I got the better end of the stick regarding our relationship. She is smarter, prettier, and more sophisticated. I had to pray, "God, please don't let me mess this up. Please help me accept the good things in my life." This was a real concern. After all, I often sabotaged myself because I couldn't accept the good things in my life. I felt like I didn't deserve them. And Olivia is definitely one of the best things that has ever happened to me.

Eventually, we got married, and I became the luckiest SOB in the world. She has cared for and about me in ways I could never have imagined.

She would go out with me when I flew the falcons. She loved it. So she studied, passed the exams, and became a certified falconer.

She liked riding my Harley with me and wanted to get her bike. She took the test at the DMV but didn't pass. But that didn't stop her. She went right back and took the test again and passed. Now she has her own bike.

She runs triathlons and a business. She is a truly remarkable woman and comes from an incredible family. Her father was a bombardier in WWII. Then he went on to be a diplomat under the Johnson administration. He did this while facing prejudice and bigotry as a Mexican American.

She grew up in Washington, DC, and all over the world. She was appointed to the Bureau of Land Management and ran a political campaign. Where we come from could not be more different.

Before we married, I said, "You know, many people will always know me as a drug trafficker and criminal, especially the politicians we will be around. Are you okay with that?"

She said, "That isn't who you are now. I don't care about all the other stuff." She loves and supports me despite knowing where I come from.

One time, early in our marriage, I left to trap falcons up in the mountains. That was legal back then, but you could only do it at a certain time of the year. It was my birthday, and I felt slightly abandoned because no one was making any kind of deal out of it. So I packed up my gear and left to do something I liked to do.

I was busy doing my thing when I got a phone call from Olivia. "Where are you?" she asked. "I'm out trapping falcons." "Really? I wanted to bring you out to dinner for your birthday." "I'll come back," I said, though I didn't really want to leave. "No, you stay."

I stayed and finished what I was doing, but the entire drive home, I kept going over and over what I had done. I got myself really spun up.

When I got home, I said, "I don't know how to do this. How can I can change to be a better husband?"

Olivia sat there for a minute and replied, "The fact you asked is enough. I like who you are. I don't want you to change."

We were both constantly on the go for the first few years of our marriage. Sometimes we would only see each other when we passed in the airport. She was traveling back and forth between Washington, DC, and Albuquerque, and I was traveling all over the southwest for SkyHawk Rugs. We were so busy that we didn't even have a honeymoon!

For our second anniversary, we finally had our long-awaited honeymoon. We went to Scotland. It was a wonderful trip, and we were able to reconnect.

When Olivia left her job, she came and started running SkyHawk Rugs with me. She is an integral part of the business and how it grew. Now that I'm getting older and unable to do as much as I used to, she pretty much runs the business on her own. She does this while still caring for me when I'm recovering from surgery, caring for our horses, dogs, and birds, and still being an important part of our community.

To say I hit the jackpot when Olivia chose me is a massive understatement. She is my better half. She is the calm and stabilizing force to my chaos and constant motion. We are Yin and Yang, and together we are unstoppable.

Mike Eves

My sponsor, Mike, and I spent quite a bit of time together during those early years. I was new to being sober, and he had two years of sobriety under his belt. He knew the importance of staying busy. We had many interests in common, so hanging out came naturally.

Around this time, I met the guy who flew falcons. Man,

I thought that was the coolest thing ever. Coincidentally, he was also a former drug runner. Over the years, I have found that once people get out of the drug business and get clean, they are drawn into things like falconry. If I put on my armchair psychologist hat for a moment, I guess we are drawn to these hobbies because we look for exciting, adrenaline-inducing activities. That's probably how we got into the drug business, to begin with.

Once I found out Mike was a master falconer, we were out there flying falcons together. He taught me everything there was to know, including finding and raising hatchlings. It was yet another cool way that God gave us to bond.

Mike and I have traipsed the country several times, hunting, fishing, flying falcons, and supporting each other in sobriety. We both found a powerful, spiritual connection in nature. God used his creation to heal us and to give us the space to process our thoughts.

After a while, I started sponsoring people on their journey to sobriety. One of the guys I sponsored was Bill Long. He became good friends with Mike and me and began to join us on our adventures. We had so many good experiences together. Bill had been sober for more than thirty years when he died. Losing him the way that we did was devastating to both Mike and me.

Mike and I have been good friends for nearly forty years now. We've had our ups and downs, but the bond we created in those early years as we stayed sober is a bond of trust and loyalty that is the deepest of any relationship I know.

Rugs

I had hobbies but still needed a way to stay busy and earn money. I prayed God would provide me a job to keep me busy and sober. My only request was that it wouldn't be handing out flyers on the side of the road. God, with his infinite sense of humor, got me a job selling rugs on the roadside instead.

One day as I was walking down the street, I noticed a man selling rugs from a booth on the side of the road. I stopped and chatted with him briefly, and he offered me a job. It was the perfect job for me at the time. I was physically active while setting up the rugs and packing them back up every day, and my boss let me leave for an hour to go to my AA meetings.

Soon I was traveling with him to different events and shows, selling rugs everywhere. And I was a damn good rug salesman. I guess I got some of my Dad's selling abilities after all. Soon, this job would be the foundation for building my own business.

CHAPTER TWELVE

Interview

Kristine:

Listening to Patrick's descent into drugs and alcoholism was difficult, especially as my brother had died from an overdose a year before. I knew he would overcome his demons. However, I couldn't help but want to save him from the pain as his addiction took over his life. I wondered what his journey toward sobriety looked like to someone on the outside. Mike Eves, his first sponsor and lifelong friend, agreed to speak with me about their relationship.

Interview with Mike Eves

Mike has a soft-spoken, professional voice. Listening to him speak, I would never guess he had been one of the most prominent drug runners in the western US during the 70s and 80s.

Mike chuckled a bit: "*I remember the first time I saw Patrick at an AA meeting. Pat is a very tall guy, and he wore this tall cowboy hat, which made him look even taller. He sat in the back of the room with his back to the wall and didn't say a word. He had a look on his face that said this was not a man you wanted to* mess with. He definitely made quite an impression. We came from the same drug worlds, so I knew of him and who he was, but somehow we'd never crossed paths.

When we finally met and started talking, we realized that we shared a common goal in sobriety and shared history, if you will. Honestly, it is God's grace that we didn't know each other back in our drug days. It was better that we got to know each other through our sobriety.

The bond between us happened very quickly, not only because we were both working on our sobriety but because we enjoyed the same things. We stayed very close, and we helped each other change our lives. It was a very special time for him and me."

"One of those interests is falconry. Before meeting Pat, I was a master falconer but hadn't practiced for a long time. I got my first falcon on my 9th birthday and chased and trained falcons my whole life.

Then I got very sick and ended up in rehab. I wasn't able to practice falconry for a long time. Patrick got hooked on it somewhere early in his sobriety. He met someone that I knew pretty well. He's the one that got Patrick hooked on the sport. Then Patrick reintroduced me to it.

We had lots of wonderful times outdoors with the birds. We went all over the country. We are both very spiritual men that don't believe in coincidences. We were meant to be in each other's lives. God had it all planned perfectly. We helped each other, and as a result, we could help others. We have had quite an adventure."

"However, the early days of our friendship were hard. We were both early on in our sobriety. It wasn't like we magically became okay. We had a special relationship because I was his sponsor, and he learned from me. And later, we learned from each other. That's how AA works. We now know each other better than our own mothers knew us. You get that close.

I was 35 years old when I got sober. Suddenly everything I had ever known about myself changed. All my friends were dead, on their way to death, or in jail.

At this time in our history, our generation felt there was no tomorrow. Pat came into AA feeling the same way. He was like, "What am I going to do? This life is going to be really dull. I'm not drinking. I'm not drugging. I'm not partying. I'm not making a living the way that I used to. What the hell am I going to do? This is like the end of the line."

But I encouraged him that it wasn't the end of the line; it was just the beginning. Now that he was sober, everything would only get better. This was the time when everything we ever wanted could start to happen. We weren't able to get there before because we were so self-destructive. But now, all the lights were green, and nothing could hold us back but ourselves. Together we could do this, and we did. Then we were able to help a lot of other people."

"Soon after we met, I started Cocaine Anonymous with two other people in Albuquerque. It began with just Pat, the three of us, and a few others sitting in a room, sharing and encouraging one another. We quickly grew to about 300 people attending the meetings, professional people, wonderful people.

"Sobriety is a continual journey. You must decide to get help; it takes time and commitment to get well. It takes a willingness to accept help from other people and the program.

Recreating Patrick

I've known many people who have gotten sober, and every one of them has gotten sober with some form of spiritual help. This is a spiritual process too. People forget that. You have to allow people to help you and ask for help. It's a hard time. But no matter what, don't drink, don't use. No matter what. Get a sponsor and do all those things because it works.

It works for the people that work it. It doesn't work for the people who really want or need it; wanting and needing it isn't enough. It only works for the people who really work it. You have to put the work in!

Another thing. There is something about being outside in nature; it is healing. Patrick and I did a lot of activities outdoors together. In these beautiful natural settings, you feel in touch with yourself and your spirit. We spent a lot of time doing that. Then there was hunting, flying birds, and just driving. We drove all over the country together.

I have a picture here that I'm looking at as I talk to you. Pat took it. It's of me on my horse on one of those trips. He bought me my first horse. Then we started doing backpacking trips in New Mexico and Colorado. We had all kinds of great times fishing and hunting.

There were a lot of lumps in between. We got crossways with each other a few times. When you get that close to someone, you will have disagreements. People always fight with their brothers, and Patrick is like a brother to me. He can be volatile at times, and I can be rather sanctimonious and self-righteous." Mike laughs at himself for a moment.

"Patrick is very generous with both his time and with things. He was always buying gifts, and he was very conscientious. He would always bring you something back when he went on a trip. I always liked that. He is very thoughtful like that.

But Patrick can change on a dime. Certain things about ourselves go deep, even back to childhood—things we don't even recognize about ourselves. We don't even know they are there until they are right on the surface, and then we blow and don't even know why. But we focused on what was important, our friendship, and didn't spend too much time on what was negative. We were sideways with each other several times, which wasn't good. But truthfully, I don't think about those times too much. We had too many good times."

"Our history really bonded us. When you come from that world, you don't trust anyone. Our history is what got us to talk, trust, and cross that spiritual boundary that changed our lives. We are entirely different people. We have been forever. We are not the people that we used to be.

We don't take from people anymore. We help people. We believe that is why we are here. It is essential that we give back. You better give it away because it was given to you very freely. I was facing 60 years in federal prison when I got sober. And I know if they had caught up with Pat, he would have faced a significant amount of hard time too. All the people around him spent a substantial amount of time in prison. We were deep into that drug world.

I must tell you about Bill Long because he was very important to us.

In the early days, Patrick and I led NA and AA meetings at several treatment centers; Bill was a patient at one. I remember he came to his first meeting wearing these funny pajamas and little socks. We took to him, and he took to us. I sponsored Pat, and Pat sponsored Bill."

"Bill began going on our trips with us. He'd be our camp cook because he didn't hunt. But he did love fishing. The three of us used to fly fish at this extraordinary place with cabins, fishing guides, and everything.

Bill was sober for 27 o 28 years. He was getting older and started acting depressed and making rash decisions. For example, he argued with his long-time friend and boss and quit his job. Pat and I tried to keep talking to him, but he was deteriorating. The last night Pat, Olivia, and I saw him together was at a restaurant. I entered the room, and Bill turned around and said, "Oh no, not him!" Because he knew we were staging a bit of an intervention. I saw him again when I brought him to my house for Thanksgiving dinner.

The next thing we knew, he put a bullet in his head. That day, we lost a very, very dear friend. That was hard; we'd been friends for a long time.

But although I knew Bill well, I never knew him as well as Pat. Bill never shared the deep stuff with me. It was more surface-level. I couldn't tell you his kids' names or if he paid child support. There were a lot of things he just didn't talk about. It was probably different for Pat because he was Bill's sponsor. So they probably had a deeper relationship than Bill and I.

So Bill was a big part of what we had. His loss definitely hit us both hard. I still have his number on my phone, and I'd bet Pat does too."

" I like to remember all Pat and I did together. I was there when Pat shot his first deer and his first elk. It was a moonlit sky in the Via Grande, a full moon.

We were in this tranquil meadow, up in the beautiful mountains. It was just incredible for us to be together for that. We were so proud.

I don't know how many shots ago that was. But that was a long time ago. I haven't been hunting in a long time, but Pat's still chasing them around. But I was there for the first one.

You tend to grow apart when you don't spend time with people. And that has happened with Pat and me. But I can still tell you that I know Pat, and Pat knows me. And that will never change, no matter how far apart we live or how long it is before we speak to each other."

My interview with Mike was like catching a glimpse of a piece of Patrick's soul. Not many people have a friendship in life as deep, raw, and honest as Mike and Pat have had. Having a friend who stands by you and doesn't judge you, even knowing the darkest of your secrets, is a rare gift.

Interview with Pat Durrant

Pat Durrant has been Patrick's longtime friend and colleague. He was amidst grief and planning due to a death in his family but still graciously made time to speak with me. That is the kind of loyalty and friendship that Patrick inspires in others.

"I met Patrick after getting sober, but it was early in my sobriety journey. He hired me to work for SkyHawk Rugs early on. He would let me leave work for an hour a day to go to a meeting because he understood and supported my sobriety. That started a working relationship that lasted for twenty-five or so years. The business

grew into something extraordinary. I don't think we had any idea how big it would grow.

Patrick is a good friend who has positively influenced my life. Our friendship had its ups and downs, but that is to be expected when you've been friends for as many years as we have!

Patrick is a persistent and complicated man. He can be mercurial. Sometimes, we wanted to kill each other or, at the very least, hit each other with a baseball bat. But we always came back around. We've been friends for a long time, and I love him."

CHAPTER THIRTEEN

The Rug Man

"God does for me what I cannot do for myself. Every day of my life for the last 36 years has reinforced that."

- Partick Harrington

I worked for someone else selling rugs for a while. I was traveling for work for three to six months at a time. It was exhausting and took

a toll on my relationships. When I wasn't traveling, I came home exhausted and still had to deal with the minutia of running a business. It is impossible to maintain a healthy partnership when you are gone for half of the year. When you are home, you're physically and emotionally distracted.

However, it wasn't time wasted. I learned the ins and outs of the rug business and made industry contacts. I realized that I was very good at selling rugs. I sold more rugs than anyone else working for the company, including the owner. But I was never one to work for someone else. I would improve the business in many ways if I did it for myself. I was used to being the boss. Being an employee chaffed at my independent nature.

So I decided to strike out on my own and thus began Skyhawk Rugs. I borrowed twenty thousand dollars from a bank and bought a horse trailer to hitch to the back of my truck. Then I set out to buy rugs.

Though I had made numerous sales contacts through the shows I had sold at over the years, I didn't have a relationship with any manufacturers. This business is built on who you know. I contacted all the manufacturers I knew, but they said they couldn't help me.

Finally, I found a rug manufacturer willing to talk to me. I cowboyed up with my Rand cowboy hat, belt, and cowboy boots and drove to meet them at a small Mexican restaurant.

The men from the manufacturing company were walking into the restaurant at the same time I was.

One guy stopped me and said, *"I owe you an apology."*

"Why?" I was confused because I'd never met him before.

"Well, I didn't think you were real," he chuckled.

"I'm for dang sure real!" I laughed.

After we sat down, we got to business. *"Here's what we'll do; if you have five thousand dollars to spend, we can do business together."* I bought those first rugs, and Sky Hawk Rugs was born.

I started off as a gypsy rug dealer, selling rugs on the side of the road. We would drive to Coors Road in Albuquerque to set up the rugs and chairs. Then, I would get down on my knees and pray, "*God, keep me busy until they come.*" Then I would get up, straighten the rugs, and the customers started coming. And by God's grace, they are still coming thirty years later.

That's my deal. I showed up, and I still show up. When people ask me the secret to my success, I always tell them, "*Just keep showing up, and you're a success.*" I showed up seven days a week in the rain, the heat, the snow, and when the wind was blowing so hard that I had to nail the rug racks down. It didn't make a  damn bit of difference, and I just kept showing up. Some days I wouldn't sell a damn thing. On other days, I would sell five or six rugs. But I never gave up and always showed up because I was hungry.

I grew the business from there. My old boss tried to blackball me with the manufacturers. He had been in the business a long time, so he had a lot of contacts. But by then, I had a couple of manufacturers who liked dealing with me.

A manufacturer from LA kept calling me, but I didn't know if I could make the financial commitment to make it worth my while.

Finally, the owner asked me, *"Why haven't you been returning my calls? I want to do business with you."*

"I just don't know that I can make the kind of investment it would take to import yet," I told him.

But he convinced me, and I started ordering rugs from him. I would only order what I could pay for upfront, in cash. Before long, I was ordering entire shipping containers of rugs from him. People like doing business with me because I'm upfront with them.

Then, I started designing my own rugs. Before Sky Hawk Rugs, "cowboy rugs" didn't exist. You could get southwestern or Native American-styled rugs. But there were no cowboy rugs.

By God's grace and hard work, the business continued to grow, and I hired more people. We opened several storefronts and traveled to big rodeos, rug shows, and events.

One of my manufacturers told me, *"We don't make a lot of money off of you, but we make a lot of money off your designs."* I enjoy designing rugs, but I'm more of a concept artist. I usually come up with the idea and then work with one of several talented artists to create the finished design.

I traveled all over the southwest selling rugs. At first, I focused on selling rugs on street corners. I had several corners in Santa Fe, Albuquerque, Lubbok, Levitin, and many other cities. I was in Texas, Colorado, Wyoming, Montana, New Mexico, Nevada, Nebraska, Idaho, and the list goes on.

Eventually, Sky Hawk Rugs brought me all over the world. I traveled to Turkey more times than I could count. Then we branched out and hired manufacturers in Egypt and Saudia Arabia.

My contact in Egypt was well connected. They brought us to all the ancient monuments. I got to go inside the Great Pyramid of Giza and explore it. What an amazing experience!

I was the first in our group to crawl inside; everyone, including my son, was behind me. When we started exploring, I didn't realize how small the tunnels inside the pyramid were. You must get down on your hands and knees and crawl through some tunnels. I am a large man, and I'm very claustrophobic. However, I was at the head of the line, with everyone else in the group behind me. There was no way to go but forward. I started to panic, and the heat and the small space were closing in on me. But I managed to calm myself down by playing tour guide to the rest of the group. I had everyone laughing and joking around by the time we made it to the king's burial chamber.

Wow! What a sight! You are squeezing yourself like a packed sardine through these tunnels, and suddenly, you are in a massive, echoing stone chamber. There is no way to describe the feeling inside this ancient, majestic space. It was truly a once-in-a-lifetime experience.

My friend had access to other closed archeological sites that were only available to archeologists and Egyptologists. We toured a tomb with hieroglyphs depicting what they thought could be an ancient battery! We genuinely do not understand just how advanced our ancient ancestors were.

On one trip to Egypt, Olivia and I met a young woman in the market who offered her services as a tour guide. She showed us around for a bit and invited us back to her family's home. I called a friend on my satellite phone and told them where we were heading. Though I trusted the tour guide, someone should always know where you are going in a foreign country. If something happens to you, the authorities will have a place to start looking.

She invited us to her family home, and we spent a fantastic evening with her parents and siblings. We learned much about their culture from them. I cherish the memories from that visit.

I toured the rug factory in Egypt, where they produced our rugs. Watching the manufacturing process where your idea goes from a concept on paper to something you can feel and hold in your hand was cool. At SkyHawk Rugs, we only use the best quality fibers and dyes in our rugs. They are designed to hold up to be walked on by people and pets, be shampooed, and still look amazing. And we only use manufacturers dedicated to the same level of quality.

It is vital that I know this business inside and out, from start to finish. I tour every factory where our rugs are made. This commitment to quality has paid off. After I toured the first factory, I noticed a twenty percent increase in sales. We have been in business long enough that we have multi-generational customers. I am proud that we make a product that people love.

Sometimes, I can get overwhelmed by our success. On a trip to Riyadh, Saudi Arabia, I met with a manufacturer at The Capital, the tallest building in Riyadh at the time. I walked into the building and stood in front of the elevator. I was with Samir of the United Weavers. He was guarded by two tall, large black European guards. They were impressive; I wouldn't want to take them on!

I became overwhelmed with the feeling that I was unworthy of being there. At that moment, I was the poor kid from Indiana wearing ill-fitting hand-me-downs and eating stale donuts to curb the hunger pains in my stomach. I felt myself spiraling down into a pit of self-doubt. Who did I think I was fooling in my thousand-dollar hat and boots?

But then it hit me; I earned this. I worked damn hard and built a business that people respected. They respected me! I deserved to be here, at this moment, in this palatial tower, meeting the powerful men I was meeting. I felt my worth more deeply than ever when I stepped off the elevator.

CHAPTER FOURTEEN

Parental Healing

"I don't have to apologize for things I don't say. I hate apologies, so I hold my thoughts."

- Patrick Harrington

My relationship with my parents was always complicated, to put things mildly. The dysfunction I witnessed and was subjected to as a child impacted my psyche and later actions.

But no matter how messed up our childhood, there comes a point where what you do and experience is on you, not your parents. You become an adult and make your own successes and failures.

As you grow and heal, you must learn to forgive the fallible humans who raised you, no matter how shitty a job they did. I am so grateful that I could have a good relationship with my parents before they passed.

Mom

My mom fought the brutal battle of sobriety and won. She got sober in her early forties and stayed sober. She dedicated the rest of her life to God, charity, and the Catholic church. She ran several homes for unwed mothers, loving them and teaching them how to be the kind of mothers she wished she had been for us.

Our local paper did a news story about her journey to sobriety. She became an inspiration and mentor to many people for the last half of her life.

Her psychological health stabilized to a large degree after she got sober. She was not perfect, but she did her best to make amends for the past.

I was able to spend time enjoying her company and doing the kind of fun things we never could when I was a kid. I would fly her to New Mexico. We would go to live shows and fine restaurants and enjoy each other's company.

Her mental acuity began to slip right before she died, and she became challenging to be around. She would say harsh things and became difficult to handle. One day, I had had enough. I snapped and let her have it, telling her exactly what I thought and felt. I had pushed down more hurt over the years than I realized and had hurts from my childhood that had never healed.

I was done with her, I thought to myself! I was now a grown-ass man and didn't need to deal with her crap.

But eventually, I calmed down and realized that she was my mom despite everything, and I didn't have much time left with her. I picked up the phone and called her. She apologized, and I forgave her. Then I apologized for some of what I said.

It wasn't long after that conversation that my mom passed away. I'm at peace knowing we had forgiven and reconciled before she died.

Dad

During my entire childhood, I looked up to my dad. I wanted to be like him. I lied, covered things up for him, and followed in his criminal footsteps. However, I became a much better criminal than he ever was. This gave me a twisted sense of pride before I got sober and got my life together.

But in some ways, my Dad did the most damage to me as a child. He taught me how to skirt the law, introduced me to his wanna-be mob friends, and exposed me to some twisted sexual situations, like our night with the same prostitute.

As a kid, I idolized my dad. As an adult, I became my dad. Once I got sober, I had to do a lot of self-reflection, therapy, and healing regarding my complicated relationship with him.

But I always loved him, and we remained close. He even lived with me for a time before he died. He was always proud of the success that I had achieved.

I could take him on trips and do fun things that we had been too poor to do growing up. And like with my mom, we had a good relationship when he passed.

I am reconciled with how our earthly time together ended. I know my parents regretted many of their choices and how they acted while we were growing up. However, they both grew and evolved as people. I learned that anyone can change and grow no matter how old they are by watching them.

Gabriel

For most of my son's childhood, I was an addict and drug dealer. I exposed him to people and things that I find chilling when I look back. I loved him, but addicts are incapable of making good decisions.

There were good times. From the time he was a small tot, he rode on my bike with me. He knew the feel of the open road almost before he knew the feel of the ground under his feet. To this day, our love for motorcycles and riding is one of the things we share. It is a special bond. I also  provided for him. I never wanted him to be without the way that I was as a child.

In reality, his mom, Connie, mostly raised him. And she did a great job. But I regret many things about the kind of father I was to him when he was young.

Once I got sober, I made amends the best that I could. But at the time, he was in the middle of his own addiction. It took many years before we were both in a place where our relationship could begin to heal.

But I have always loved him. One time, he was missing, and no one could find him. We'd looked everywhere, hospitals, his friends, the drug house, but we could not find him. I suited up and got ready to go to some really dark places, the kind of places inside of myself that I had left behind years before, because I was going to find my son, no matter what it cost me.

Gabriel came home before I had to return to the person I used to be. I told him when he returned, "You have no idea the places I was ready to go to and the things I was ready to do to find you. Please don't make me go there again."

Gabriel has his own story of overcoming addiction and sobriety. I am proud of the man he is today. He is a hardworking father, a Knight of Columbus in the Catholic church, and a man of deep faith. Our relationship may not be perfect, but it is strong. I am blessed that God has helped us restore the relationship that addiction robbed us of.

CHAPTER FIFTEEN

Mental Health

"I decided early on in my sobriety that I didn't want to be a victim or a survivor of the abuse I suffered or inflicted in my past. I wanted to live the best life that I could. So I have."

- Patrick Harrington

Once I got sober, I had no choice but to address my mental health. My whole life, I had pushed all the trauma, pain, loss, anger, and fear deep inside. When I couldn't push it down further, I drank and did drugs to keep it down. Every painful memory, dark feeling, and irrational fear began to resurface. All the losses that I had never grieved began to overwhelm me. Sobriety had made it impossible to ignore the PTSD, depression, and anxiety I had avoided acknowledging my entire life.

Today, there is a slow shift towards acknowledging and accepting mental health issues. However, I was born and raised in a time when they were not talked about. Because my mother was in and out of institutions during childhood, I felt shame and secrecy about my psychological and emotional struggles. Strong people deal with their crap themselves was my mentality for much of my life.

But AA taught me that kind of thinking was bullshit. An essential step towards sobriety is humbling yourself by honestly admitting your struggles, asking for help, and creating a support network that accepts and holds you accountable.

Because I spent so many years in the throes of severe addiction, I needed a lot of support. I spent many years attending an intensive outpatient program. That program helped me delve into the issues that had haunted me my entire life.

Suicide

I always assumed I would die from a gunshot wound to the head. Whether I or someone else delivered the kill shot depended on the day and my state of mind. People are often surprised to find out that I fight suicidal ideations. I am a man that embraces life with both hands and tries to wring every novel and exciting experience from it that I am able. But I can also plummet to the depths of depression, my head swimming in a sea of anxiety and hopelessness in the blink of an eye.

Over the years, I have learned coping mechanisms that help me fight off these dark times. My faith has held me fast and comforted me more than I can count. Because I have lost people I loved to suicide, I have an intimate understanding of how that loss devastates those left behind. I have no desire to do that to my family and friends. I refuse to give in to the darkness. So I go to personal therapy and support groups, take the medication my psychiatrist prescribes, and keep myself busy so

I don't have time to think. I do it all because I do not want to go down that dark path like my friend Bill.

Bill Long was one of the first people I sponsored in AA. He, Mike Eaves, and I were like the three amigos. We did everything together. Bill was a good man, but he had his demons like all of us do. A year or so before he died, he started mentally and emotionally deteriorating. Mike and I kept reaching out to him, but he wouldn't hear us.

The demons finally caught up to him. He took his 22 and ended his life. He knew he could reach out to Mike or me, but he didn't. I'm still a little pissed at him for that. Losing him cut deep, I'm not going to lie. I gave the eulogy at his funeral. Man, that was tough. I still miss him; he was like a brother to me.

Suicide steals too many good men and women every year, especially our veterans. Twenty-two veterans a day take their own lives. Think about that. More than 8,000 people a year survive the brutalities of battle and military life only to come home and commit suicide. This is unacceptable!

Between 20%-40% of our war veterans suffer from mental health issues. But many do not seek help because they  fear it will negatively affect their career or that their family and friends will judge them. Even among those who seek help, over 53% do not get adequate treatment. We as a nation are failing our heroes, the men, and women who put everything on the line for us. We must do better.

The semi-colon has become a symbol of hope for many who have faced suicidal ideations or attempted suicide. The semi-colon is used to continue a sentence instead of ending it. Like the semi-colon, we have continued when our stories could have ended.

I have a tattoo of the semi-colon. On the good days, it is a reminder that I have fought long and hard to get to where I am today and live the beautiful life I have. On the bad days, it reminds me that my story is not over.

Daniel

In my darkest times, God has always been there for me. I think I have always had a guardian angel. Still, I didn't notice all the interventions, roadblocks, and signs until I got sober. I was too hardened and cold before sobriety to see anything other than what I needed at that moment. Once I got sober, I became a much nicer person. I became aware of higher consciousness and mindful of God and spirituality. I believe in God. I don't pretend to have it all figured out or know how it all works. I just know that there is a God, and he is why I am still here. He does for me what I can't do for myself.

Over the years, I have known many people who believed in God. My older sister Mary was one of them. She also had a guardian angel looking over her. She fought cancer for over twenty years. The disease took her breasts and one of her legs above the knee. But she never lost hope and always believed. The doctors didn't think she would make it as long as she did. But her guardian angels kept that cancer from taking her before her time for twenty years.

I remember the day I realized I had a guardian angel. I was on a hunting trip with a guide. I had separated from the group to hunt alone for a bit. It had been a good trip, though I was in a bit of pain due to my arthritis. And as suddenly as that, I was drowning in a bottomless pit of depression and anxiety. It is hard to describe the feeling if you've never been there. It is as if every bit of sunshine is gone. All you can see is the darkness swirling around your head—thoughts of hopelessness, despair, shame, guilt, and sorrow claw at you from all sides. You try desperately to fight them off, but there comes a moment where the only way out, the only end to the torment that you can see, is the sweet stillness of death. I was ready to end it all right there, but instead, I prayed. I said, *"God, if you need me to stay here, then you are gonna need to make it real obvious, real fast."* It was then that I felt the presence of my guardian angel. Suddenly, the demons in my mind quieted, and I felt at peace. I asked the presence what his name was, but I never got an answer. I figured he was part of AA, Angels Anonymous. *"Since you haven't answered, I'll call you Daniel."*

I have kept Daniel busy over the years, that's for sure. Once on my way home from a Vegas rug show, I was exhausted, so one of my employees volunteered to drive my truck and tow the trailer. This was her first time pulling the big horse trailer we used to transport our rugs.

I was sitting in the passenger's seat and giving her pointers on how to tow safely, and she was doing pretty well. Then suddenly, she swerved, causing the trailer to start fishtailing. I knew just as sure as I was sitting there that we would be crashing and the truck would roll. I told the girl driving, "*We are going to crash. Don't tense up. It will make it worse.*" Then we crashed through the guard rail, and the truck was rolling over and over. I felt my body being flung forward toward the windshield. I remember thinking, "*Well, this is it. I'm not walking away from this one.*" Then I felt two hands holding me back against my seat. When I say I felt these hands, I mean I physically felt them. Daniel was there, and he saved my life yet again.

The first responders had to use the jaws of life to cut us out of the truck. The truck and the trailer were an unrecognizable mangled mass of metal; nothing was left of them.

Olivia followed behind us in another car and watched in horror as the accident occurred. She unquestionably has some PTSD from that whole experience. We both do. It took me a long time to ride in a car where someone else was driving.

It was a miracle that both my employee and I survived the accident. I was pretty banged up and required surgery. Still, by the grace of God,

Daniel's intervention, and Olivia nursing me back to health, I made it through.

Diagnoses and Help

I have spent a lot of time in therapy throughout the years. All of the therapists, support groups, and psychiatrists have helped me understand my PTSD and depression and begin to manage them. But I had to do a lot of painful work to get to this point.

I was diagnosed with complex PTSD because of all the trauma I experienced over the years. One of the significant contributors to my PTSD was the attack I experienced while stationed at Fort Knox. For years, I had a recurring nightmare where I was naked, hiding in the brush with a gun, and I wasn't sure if I would take out whoever was hunting me or myself. The one thing I did know was that I would never let them get me. I scrambled to find a gun and shot myself in the head.

One of my therapists recently explained that the attack was traumatizing for more reasons than the violent beating by other soldiers and the trauma of having a gun held to my head. I was naked in a space that was supposed to be safe, with men who were supposed to have my back when I was attacked. They got me at my most vulnerable in every way. My therapist diagnosed me with MST (military sexual trauma). I still carry a gun all the time. Whenever I go out, I sit with my back to the wall and don't trust people easily.

One of the coping mechanisms that I developed over the years was having what I called "the committee" in my head. When making a decision, my brain gave each thought its own voice. It is hard to describe to others, but I have talked to other alcoholics who experienced something similar. Now that I've been sober for so long, I don't hear the committee as often as I used to. My psyche has healed enough to think clearly without personifying my thoughts.

The road to having better mental health has not been easy. It has taken commitment, humility, honesty, and a willingness to seek help. I am grateful to my many therapists who have helped me live a healthier life over the years. I still have my bad days, but they are much less frequent than they used to be.

Northwest Battle Buddies and My Boy *combat.*" I have to fight that particular demon off quite often.

I went through the application process for Battle Buddies and was approved! I drove to Oregon, towing the horse trailer with a bunk area. I rented a campsite which became my home for the next six weeks.

Northwest Battle Buddies is a fantastic faith-based organization. They train their dogs from puppies. Then, when the dogs are ready, they hold training programs with the prospective owners. They match each person with their dog individually. I was paired with my amazing black lab, Wrigley.

You have to commit to doing the entire six-week training program. During that time, you and your dog learn to work together. And make no mistake, it is work. I've trained dogs in the past for falcon hunting. So I wasn't a complete novice to the concepts of dog training. But when I was in the program, I was there to learn. I was humble and did what they told me. These people know their stuff! Training a service dog is very different than teaching a hunting dog. I learned everything I could from the experts at Northwest Battle Buddies. That knowledge has made my experience with Wrigley that much more productive.

Wrigley knows he is on the job when he has his vest. And his job is to be in tune with me and calm me down. He takes it seriously. When the vest comes off, he runs around, plays, and is a regular dog. But even then, he knows me. Wrigley goes everywhere with me, including sleeping in my room with me. More than once, when I was having a nightmare, he awakened me by cuddling up next to me or licking my face.

Wrigley is a part of every aspect of my life. He has become the mascot of my local veteran's PTSD group. Rug shows increase my anxiety, but Wrigley is on the job. He has become the unofficial mascot of SkyHawk Rugs because everyone who meets him falls in love with him. He even does charity events for veterans with me. Wrigley has improved my life, and I'm grateful for him and the excellent work of Battle Buddies.

CHAPTER SIXTEEN

Learning to Live

"I'm not too proud to pick up pennies off the ground. When I find one that is heads up, I leave it there to bring someone good luck. When I find one face down, I turn it over and leave it to bring another person good fortune."

- Patrick Harrington

Getting sober allowed me to finally have a life. I was too paranoid to truly live all the years I was selling drugs, drinking, and drugging. So I crept from stash house to stash house, stayed in the shadows at parties, and obsessed over who was after me.

Sobriety opened life's doors, and I wanted to experience it all! I trained horses, birds, and dogs. I fly falcons and RC airplanes. I have traveled the world, driven fast boats, and hunted on every continent. Hell, I even started a marble collection!

Sobriety has been the gift that keeps giving in the best of ways. I don't want my focus on the struggles of the journey to maintain my sobriety to overshadow the amazing life that I have lived.

As I am getting older, I can look back and honestly say that I have experienced almost everything my heart desired to do, no matter how cockamamie the idea may have been. Being sober does not mean you

suddenly lead a boring, monkish existence. There are no rules about what you can or can't do while sober except one: Don't drink or use. Other than that, the world is your oyster! And I have experienced it all. And as Sinatra would say, "I did it my way!" I have no regrets that I took life by the balls and have squeezed every exciting experience out of it that I could. I've lived life to the fullest, and I wouldn't change a second of that.

To record every adventure I have had since getting sober would be a book all its own. But I will share a few highlights from the places I went and the things I have done.

Mongolia

After getting sober, I met a man that taught me how to fly falcons. I truly loved the sport and eventually became a Master Falconer in my own right. I still have a few hawks though I can no longer hunt with them as I used to due to arthritis and back injuries.

Recreating Patrick

One of the highlights of my life is my trip to Mongolia to learn to fly Eagles using traditional methods. For several weeks I lived with the

Kazakh people in the Altai Mountains. The Kazakh tribes live where Russia, China, Mongolia, and Kazakhstan meet. For centuries they have hunted on horseback using Golden Eagles trained by hand. They still use the ancient training and hunting methods passed down from generation to generation.

Though many Kazakhs have migrated to the cities to access education, healthcare, and jobs, some have chosen to live the traditional hunting and herding lifestyle as ancient as the people themselves.

Though I was a stranger, the Kazakh people brought me in as part of their family. I stayed in a traditional yurt and ate meals with my host's family. This presented a challenge because rice is a staple of their diet, and I never eat rice. Once, while a cook in the army, I got to work early to cook breakfast. I went to the trashcan to peel potatoes, only to find that someone had left chicken bones in the bin the night before. By the time I arrived in the morning, the industrial-sized can had inches of maggots writhing on top of each other. Since that day, I can't look at rice, much less eat it. However, I explained that I couldn't eat rice, and my hosts were very gracious. I always bring my own food supply when I travel, like protein bars and nuts. So I knew I wouldn't go hungry. But they had plenty of other food options, which I enjoyed.

I learned so much in my time with them. The Kazakh men start teaching their sons how to train Golden Eagles early. These peoples' bonds with their birds are unlike anything I had seen before. Golden Eagles are majestic animals. They have a wingspan of over six feet long and razor-like claws. When diving down for prey, they can reach nearly ninety miles an hour. Yet, these fierce hunters are carried, almost cradled, by the men who care for them.

Training a Golden Eagle is a three or four-year process. By the time they are ready to go on hunts, they recognize the voice and commands

of their trainer. They become a part of the family for ten years. Then, the trainer brings the bird high into the mountains and releases it to live in the wild for the rest of its natural life (up to thirty years). It is a hard separation for both the trainer and the bird, but it is in the best interest of the eagle. Kazakhs have great reverence for their birds. It is a symbiotic relationship, not one of ownership. In this way, the eagles reproduce naturally in the wild.

I have made it a tradition to leave my AA sobriety chips in the special places I travel to. It is an essential ritual to acknowledge that I'm having these incredible experiences because of my sobriety. I left one of my chips in the mountains of Mongolia. Now a piece of me will always be there.

On my trip, I also saw a lot of Mongolia. I love seeing new places, meeting people, and learning about their cultures. I met a man while touring the city. He loved my cowboy hat. I only had one hat with me, but I told him I would send it to him once I got home. I kept that promise. So if you meet a man with a big cowboy hat selling wares at a stall in a Mongolian marketplace, tell him I said hi.

Africa

A while back, I was at the SCI show in Las Vegas. I was wandering around, poking my head in vendor booths, and chatting with friends I had made. There would be a banquet and auction that night, but I hadn't planned on attending. Then I ran into an old friend who invited me to the banquet again; she even gave me the tickets! Of course, I said I would go.

While at the banquet, I met a young man who was a hunting guide in Africa. He was auctioning off one of his hunting trips. I had always wanted to go to Africa and liked the guy, so I bid on the trip and won it.

I went home and told Olivia that I had won the trip. She said, *"What about me?"* I didn't think she would want to go with me. *"I would love for you to come if you would like to,"* I said, genuinely pleased that she wanted to come. *"I want to go,"* she said. And that was that we were going to Africa.

It was a fantastic trip. The tour company had a luxurious chalet for Olivia and me to stay in and a beautiful lodge for meals and entertainment. I bought the trip for a song back in Vegas but made up for it by spending a lot of money there. I made a good friend and shot some animals, though I missed kudu at 100 yards. It was a 500-yard trek back to the truck after that miss. Talk about being embarrassed. I made excuses about the sun being in my eyes, but that was bullshit. The truth is that I missed the shot. The guide said, *"Don't worry about it, man. It happens all the time because they are such majestic creatures."* He was right about that. They are magnificent.

I saw a warthog the next day and dropped it with no problem. So I redeemed myself a bit. We had such a great time that we returned the following year. Olivia had hurt her ankle and could not walk much on the first trip. The following year, we made up for it by doing a lot of fun extra things.

I was determined to get a kudu when we returned to the hunting lodge. Olivia's ankle was fine on this trip, and she wanted to come along for the hunt. The hunter on the trip didn't want anyone else to go. However, I had paid a small fortune for the trip. If my wife wanted to come along, she would come along. I'm not particularly eager to push my weight around like that, but I will do what I need to do when it comes down to it. When it was all said and done, Olivia went with us.

Recreating Patrick

We tracked kudo over 50,000 acres of private land but didn't see a single kudu for two or three days. The guide was nervous because the hunt was ending, but we finally caught up to one. The guide and I had to leave everyone behind for the last 100 yards because it was covered in thick brush. But then I saw it. I aimed and fired. Most animals give a death bellow when they die, but kudus shed a single tear. It was a spiritual moment. I respect every animal that I hunt. Every time I kill one, I thank them that I met them at that point in their lives; it was destiny between them and me at that particular moment.

After leaving the hunting lodge, we went to Sossusvlei to see the petrified dunes in Nambia. They are magnificent, massive dunes that nature has painted in gorgeous hues of orange and red. My friend drove us up to the top of one of the dunes on his four-wheeler. What a breathtaking view! Olivia and I were taking pictures when I noticed my friend letting the air pressure out of his tires. He laughed and told me a story.

"I brought my friend who hunts grizzly bears up here once." I asked him, "Do you ever get scared?" He said, "No." I told him the same thing I'm about to say to you, "You're going to be scared now!"

My friend laughed again, and we all piled back into the four-wheeler. My seatbelt was stuck and wouldn't snap on, and we were driving straight down this 1300-foot-tall dune! Oh my God! Everyone was screaming their asses off. It was absolutely thrilling!

Then we took a boat ride out on the ocean and had the best oysters I have ever eaten. They are small, but they are meaty and delicious. We truly enjoyed ourselves on this trip.

On my third trip to Africa, Olivia didn't want to go. I was going to hunt cape buffalo, which are dangerous game, and I was staying in a primitive camp. By primitive, I mean we stayed in tents without running water or electricity. It was you, the guides, and nature. That level of roughing it is not Olivia's cup of tea.

I had bought this trip at an auction three years before. I was scheduled to go but had to cancel the trip because I had to have a pacemaker put in my heart. I rescheduled for the following year but then had to cancel again because I had a serious car accident on my way back from Las Vegas.

Finally, in the third year, I was able to go. I was weak and a little discombobulated, but I made it there!

I had always wanted to hunt a cape buffalo. They are not very tall, but they are huge. Some of the bulls can weigh up to 1900 pounds! The males' horns are larger and thicker than the females'. They can grow three and a half feet wide and have a shield plate covering their foreheads. This shield only completely forms once they reach maturity at seven years old.

It was a good hunt. The first cape buffalo I shot ran off into the cane. We tracked him for a long time because you never want to leave a wounded animal in the wild to suffer. But we weren't able to find him.

I had only paid for one buffalo on that trip, but since I wanted to bring back the trophy, I paid to hunt another.

While hunting in the cane, we encountered two cape buffalo one morning. They were "dagga boys." Dagga boys are older male cape buffalo pushed out of the herd by younger males. They no longer breed and live a mostly solitary existence for the rest of their lives. The word dagga means mud. Cape Buffalos love to spend a great deal of time in the mud, trying to stay cool in the African heat.

We could barely make them out. I aimed at the one for which I had the best shot. But even then, I couldn't even see his tips. But I got off the shot, and he started bellowing. I moved forward, silent and careful. This is the most dangerous part of a hunt. You never know what a wounded animal might do. If that buffalo decided to charge, you better pray for a miracle. I got closer and got off another shot, and bam! He went down. At that moment, a weight I didn't even know I was carrying lifted off my shoulder. For three years, I had been waiting to meet this buffalo. Three years of surgeries and sitting in a damn chair recovering and fighting depression. This buffalo was about thirteen years old. He was covered in scars from gators attacking him as he crossed the river. This tough son of a gun gave his life to succumb to me at that moment in time. It was a very emotional and healing moment for me.

You can't field dress a cape buffalo because you must bring the whole buffalo to the tribal leaders. They get the meat of anything hunted on their land. So you have to move the entire animal, which is no easy feat, as buffalo weigh up to 1200 pounds.

We used the winch on the jeep to move this big-ass buffalo. As the winch was slowly reeling him towards the jeep, it broke. It flew through the air, landed on the top of the jeep, and dented it. The camp owner was mad and swearing up a blue streak because it was his personal vehicle.

There were six of us on that hunt. So all six of us were on the ass end of this big bulking cape buffalo trying to lift him into the back of the jeep. I was still weak from surgery and had my titanium knee, but somehow we got the job done. I'm sure we were quite the sight should anyone have seen us.

I've hunted all over the world. I've hunted water buffalo in Australia, musk ox in Greenland, and mountain goats in Alaska, to name a few. I have so many exciting tales that I could tell from each trip. Every hunt I go on teaches me something new about myself and nature. I have been blessed to experience so much of God's creation.

Mount Ararat

I was in Turkey with Samir on a business venture with Olivia. Though I have traveled the world and seen many unique sites, I found the trip Olivia and I took to Mount Ararat particularly meaningful.

We journeyed up the mountain and saw what some experts claim are the anchor stones from Noah's Ark. Our guide was a local man with a fascinating life story.

On our way up the mountain, we passed some prisoners working along the side of the road. He stopped and chatted with the guards and a few of the prisoners. When he returned to the car, he explained that he had been in prison with four other men for murder. While in prison, he became a doctor and had a spiritual awakening. Now he had committed his life to serving God and finding the ark.

The locals claim to know exactly where the Ark is because the knowledge has been passed down over the generations. He pointed to the area of the mountain where they say it rests. But I was still recovering from surgery and was not up to doing the climb.

I was deeply moved by the experience and had a spiritual awakening of my own. Years before I finally reached Mount Ararat, I had seen a documentary about Noah's Ark. I tried to join the expedition they discussed in the show. I had just gotten sober and was getting more spiritual. This felt like a step I needed to take in that journey.

However, the leader said it was too late because I needed a passport. I was disappointed and said to myself, "I WILL go, and if I die before, I ask God to take me there before bringing me to heaven."

Though I couldn't go when I wanted to, I was finally there. Standing on the mountain all those years later reminded me that it is never too late to achieve our dreams. I left one of my sobriety chips on the mountain as an offering of gratitude for the life that I have lived.

Tattoos

I have always been drawn to the visual arts. I went to college for photography, which has been a lifelong passion. I enjoy designing unique, artistic rugs for Skyhawk Rugs. I have found and supported local artists all over the globe while I travel.

One of my favorite forms of artistic expression is tattoos. I got my first tattoo two years ago at 68 years old. I had wanted a tattoo for a long time, but it was important that I blend in and not draw negative attention to myself. Once I got sober, I was a respectable businessman. Back in those days, respected business people didn't have tattoos. But something happens when you get older. You stop giving a care about any B.S. and do whatever the hell you want to do. So at 68 years old, I found myself going under the tattoo artist's needle for the first time.

I remember showing Olivia the sketch of the first tattoo I got. She said, *"Who got that?"* I just looked at her for a minute. *"You? You got the tattoo?"* she asked incredulously. *"Yup, I sure did,"* I told her nonchalantly. *"Well, let me see it,"* she seemed excited. Once she saw the Mongolian Eagle, she was impressed. But when I came home with my second and third tattoos, she was less than enthusiastic. *"You're getting manic with this,"* she said with a bit of edge. *"There are a lot of things I don't know, but one thing that I do know is that I don't need your permission to get a tattoo,"* I responded matter-of-factly. Olivia has been supportive ever since. When I get home, she always says, *"Let me see what you got."* She never knows what to expect because my tattoos, much like who I am, have little rhyme or reason for someone looking at them from the outside. I just get an idea of what I want, have an artist sketch it, and put it where it best fits.

Since then, I haven't stopped. I now have more than 30 tattoos, and I have no intention of stopping anytime soon!

When I first got sober, I bought a boat and jet skis. I rode horses, flew falcons, trained dogs, traveled, and enjoyed life like never before. I was and am so appreciative of life and all the wonders that it offers. I want to live big and experience it all. So I don't drink, go to my meetings, and take the pills I'm prescribed. I remember all the fantastic things I've experienced since getting sober on the dark days, and those memories help me through.

CHAPTER SEVENTEEN

Hell's Orignal Angel

"Treat me good; I'll treat you better. Treat me bad, and I'll treat you worse."

- Sonny Barger

I have traveled to exotic and unique places and met many amazing people through my travels.

Sonny Barger is one of the people I was blessed to know and call my friend. Sonny founded the original Oakland chapter of Hell's Angels. Most people know him through his many television and movie appearances, his books, or because of his position within the Hell's Angels.

The first time I met Sonny, he invited me to visit his home. After reading about something he was doing for veterans, I sent him the Rodeo Rider rug, the first rug I ever designed, and the Motorcycle rug.

I never expected to hear from him, but he called me to thank me and invited me to visit him at his house. I was honored to have been invited but didn't know what to expect.

Here was this legend, someone bigger than life, asking me to visit his home. When I arrived, he was so down-to-earth and funny; he immediately put me at ease. After shooting the breeze for a while, Sonny told me to follow him because he had something to do. He brought me outside to the flag pole. As the sun set, he reverently took the flag down, folded it, and held it close to his heart. At that moment, I knew this was a man I needed to get to know. As a fellow veteran, his love for this country spoke more about his character than any words ever could.

Sonny and I didn't meet as young men. By the time we became friends, we had both lived long enough that we had nothing to prove. The times I cherish most are hanging out at his house and listening to his stories. We shared an understanding that comes from living life flat out, never holding back, and being at peace with all you have achieved.

Even though I'm not a Hell's Angel, I've ridden with Sonny, a rare honor. People claim to know him or try to get close to him because of his fame or notoriety. They know him for his outlaw reputation. But that isn't the relationship that we had. Although we undoubtedly shared some similarities in our pasts, we bonded over everyday life. I admired Sonny's deep sense of patriotism and commitment to our veterans. The Hell's Angels protected the Vietnam veterans from protestors returning home from war. They still honor our fallen heroes by lining the entire funeral procession route to ensure that our brother or sister-in-arms gets the peaceful funeral they deserve. Sonny raised a lot of money for veteran charity organizations because he himself is a veteran.

Like all of us, Sonny has his share of regrets and learned a lot over his 82 years. He once said, *"I used to think I was such a smart guy. Then one day, I thought, "If I'm so smart, why am I sitting in prison?"* He started to change his lifestyle after that moment of clarity.

What he regretted the most was smoking for so much of his life. He had throat cancer and a tracheostomy. This gave him a throaty rumble of a voice that inexorably represents Sonny in my memory.

Sonny sent me a gold invitation to the 60th anniversary of the Hell's Angels. I later learned he only sent out five of those special invitations. I was extremely honored that he had included me in those five. There was a formal reception on Friday night, and the next night was a less formal event only for Hell's Angels. Sonny asked me to attend the Hell's Angels-only event as well. If you don't know biker culture, you may not understand how much of an honor that was. But it was him treating me as one of his brothers. That evening Sonny had his wife Zee find me among 500 Hells Angles at the Oakland Clubhouse so he could introduce me to Tobie Levingston, the founder, and president of the East Bay Dragons. Also known as the Black Dragons, they are the country's oldest all-black motorcycle club. I was between two American legends!

Several years ago, I visited the motorcycle museum in Sturgis. While there, I saw they were raising funds for ongoing projects by selling engraved bricks

that would be laid in the walkways. I purchased several, one celebrating my sobriety, one for SkyHawk Rugs, and one for my friend Sonny. It seemed only right that a man who contributed so much to

LEGENDARY SONNY BARGER VETERAN AND FREEDOM FIGHTER RIDE FREE

motorcycle culture should be represented in that walkway.

PATRICK H
CA AA B DAY
ALB NM 1986

The last time I saw Sonny was at his California house. We were in his garage, going through his memorabilia and shooting the breeze. Then he sat down and put a blanket over his lap. He chuckled and said, *"When I was younger, I'd ride my bike through a town, and I'd see some old guy sitting on his porch with a blanket on his lap, just living his life. After I got prostate cancer, I understood why they did that. It's comfortable. Now I'm the old guy sitting around with a blanket on my lap."*

Blanket or no blanket, there was no slowing Sonny down. When he turned 81, he bought himself a new Victory. He joked that when he got too old to ride, he would go out and get himself arrested and let the prison take care of him. It was a big joke because he had a wonderful wife who took excellent care of him until the end.

Sonny passed away this summer. His wife, Zee, honored me by asking that I speak at his memorial service. This is what I said.

I am honored to be invited to share a few words about Sonny here at his memorial service at Stockton Speedway. I want to honor his patriotism and our friendship. Sonny was an American legend in the MC world. To many, he was a criminal; to others, he was an icon of freedom. His last words were, "Keep your head up high, stay loyal, remain free, and always value honor."

As a Knights Templar, the statement rings true.... I am a child of God, as was Sonny. I only asked God to show Sonny the heart I had for our friendship, which was a bit different than others, and to share my understanding of life. I prayed for years that he would come to see God's grace.

As I continue to work with Veterans, he will always be in my thoughts as an American Legend on many levels. His Patriotism for the Country was evident, and he spoke about it. God bless his soul."

CHAPTER EIGHTEEN

This Is My Creed

"Religion is for people who don't want to go to hell. Spirituality is for people who have already been there."

- Patrick Harrington

I have come a long way from that lonely four-year-old boy at the orphanage. I have experienced so much of life and have learned and grown through it all. The man I am now has deep convictions and faith.

Knight's Templar

Over the past three years, I have committed myself to a more profound spirituality. I have felt unworthy of God's love throughout my life, but I have begun to understand my value in Christ over the past two years. During the pandemic, I was invited to study to become a Knight's Templar. I learned so much through the studies I completed, especially about spiritual warfare and putting on the whole armor of God. When I have bad  days, I use all the skills I've learned to do spiritual warfare. Because the devil is real, and he doesn't like it when I'm out doing what God has called me to do.

In August 2021, I was honored to become a Knight of the Knight's Templar. It is one of the greatest honors of my life to be a member of a group with almost a thousand years spent fighting for righteousness as its heritage.

In 1118 A.D., Hugues de Payens, a French knight, founded the military organization that came to be known as the Knight's Templar. Knights of the order took oaths of chastity, poverty, and obedience. They did not drink, curse, or gamble and wore a simple white mantle with a red cross emblazoned upon it.

At the time, the order's mission was to protect the Christian pilgrims traveling to the Holy Land after the Crusaders had seized control from the Muslims. Though the Crusaders held Jerusalem, the pilgrims were often robbed and killed on the journey to the city. Over time, the order grew and became influential throughout the middle east

and Europe. They founded the first international banking system, owned the island of Crete, and had a fleet of ships rivaling any state navy.

Today The Knight's Templar organization is known for its charitable work in the community and its commitment to spiritual principles. I like being a part of an organization where service to our communities is a fundamental belief.

Veterans

Supporting other veterans is very important to me. Veterans' struggles with PTSD and addiction are often ignored and undertreated. Getting services through the VA is a battle. I am still fighting to receive my VA benefits for several injuries and trauma sustained while serving in the military.

Active military members often don't seek treatment for fear of career repercussions. For these reasons, outside organizations are so important for our veterans. I am proud to be a part of the Downrange Warriors organization and its Reboot program.

Downrange Warriors is an organization founded by my friend, Todd Bray. The mission of Downrange Warriors is to stop veteran suicides by supporting veterans in any way possible, including how to reintegrate into civilian life, recovering from PTSD, and addiction recovery. They offer a variety of family activities, support groups, and counseling. Because they are a faith-based group, they do not receive government funding.

Reboot is their 12-week program for veterans recovering from PTSD. Since starting Downrange Warriors and Reboot, Cody, Wyoming, and the surrounding area went from having one of the highest veteran suicide rates in the country to only one veteran suicide. I encourage any veteran reading this book to visit their website at www.downrangewarriors.com.

Northwest Battle Buddies is another great veteran organization I have used and supported. They are the organization that trained my service dog, Wrigley.

I cannot express what an amazing gift Wrigley has been in my life. I don't know how I managed life without him. He even stayed with me while I was in the hospital recovering from surgery!

Northwest Battle Buddies have the puppies fostered until they are

a year old. Then they train them for nine months and finally they train the veterans receiving the dogs on how to work with them. I cannot recommend their program enough. For more information or to support this organization go to https://www.northwestbattlebuddies.org/

I meet veterans through my travels and the rug shows we do. I wanted to let them know they are appreciated and remembered, so I created special chips to hand out to any veteran I meet. This simple gesture has opened many doors for me to meet and support fellow veterans.

Recreating Patrick

I was at a show at the Pendleton Round-up when I met a Vietnam veteran. He and I had been chatting, and I said, *"Hey, I'd like to give you one of these chips to thank you for your service."* After I handed it to him, he abruptly walked off. Afraid I had offended him, I asked his wife if he was okay. She gave me a sad smile, *"He's fine. He's still pretty sensitive about the war."* The next day he came back to the booth. *"I just wanted to say*

thank you for the chip. In the fifty years since the war, no one has ever thanked me for my service before. It meant a lot." He then walked off just as abruptly as before with tears in his eyes. I see this a lot, especially with our Vietnam vets. They were treated horribly by the public during and after the war. Many of them have never been thanked for their service to our country.

Our veterans need our support and acceptance as they struggle to overcome the deep wounds that war leaves on their bodies and psyche. Twenty-two veterans commit suicide every day. More veterans have died at their own hands than were killed in the wars of the last twenty years. I got a semi-colon tattoo for my twenty-second tattoo to remind me that my story isn't over. It also honors all the veterans that struggle with mental health issues and suicidal ideations. Tattoo Twenty-Two carries a lot of meaning for me.

My Family and Friends

Siblings

I also have a good relationship with my siblings. Mike has been with me through so much of my journey. He has seen me at my worst and my best. He makes me laugh as no other person can. My relationships with him and my two living sisters are something that I cherish.

I don't want to sound like a sentimental man. Still, the older I get, the more I understand that our relationships with family and friends are the most important thing in our lives. Possessions come and go, but we establish a lasting legacy in the memory of those we love. I have had many longtime friends and am making new friends every day. I hope I will make a good and lasting impact on their lives.

Church

I have found a wonderful church, The CMA church in Cody, Wyoming. The pastor is welcoming and loving to everyone. He is an of God that leads by example. I have been going for several years and have made friends with many people there.

A few weeks ago, I was taking Wrigley to do his business on the side of the building, but I slipped on a patch of ice and fell hard. Immediately, I was surrounded by people praying for me and getting me help. I was in the hospital for a week and then laid up at home for a while. Olivia was out of town for SkyHawk Rugs. So the church stepped in. They visited me, brought me food, and arranged for people to take Wrigley to potty while in the hospital. Of course, Wrigley stayed with me the entire time.

We are truly blessed to have such a caring and supportive church family.

AA

I still attend AA meetings wherever I go. AA has been instrumental in my sobriety. Through their program and sponsors, I first got sober, and through their continued support, I have stayed sober. Over the years, I have been sponsored, and I have sponsored many others. My sobriety will always be my top priority in life because the minute I think I don't need to worry about it anymore is the minute I open myself up to falling. I have been sober for 35 years, and I do not take a single day of that for granted.

My journey has been a twisted road with many highs and lows. But through everything, even the darkest of my days, God has watched over and protected me. I have a beautiful wife, a hard-working and loving son, and two beautiful grandchildren. I want to take those many blessings and share what I can with others.

I am proof that God doesn't make junk. No matter how hard or dark our life gets, every one of us can change directions and live life to its fullest.

CONCLUSION

Kristine:

Patrick is a unique and dynamic man that makes a lasting impression on everyone he meets. But his impact on me has been more profound. I feel as if I have watched his life unfold before me, a silent watcher from the shadows of the future. My heart broke for the abandoned four-year-old boy with the split lip in the orphanage. I laughed at the antics of the teenager who ate an entire ice cream store's worth of ice cream in one night. I cried as he experienced loss and abuse. And I wanted to intervene when he started down the road of addiction, knowing the dark places it would lead.

I have watched him pull himself out of extreme poverty by his bootstraps and sheer determination. I admired his business acumen in any venture, whether selling drugs or designing and selling rugs. I could almost feel the shakes and terrors he experienced as he detoxed and got sober. Indeed, I have been privileged to see his life through his eyes.

But then I also got an outside look at Patrick through talking to those who know him best. He asked that they be honest as they spoke to me. So they told their truths, revealing a man they greatly respected, even in his humanity.

I am honored to have been shown the many sides of Patrick: the boy, the hardworking teenager, the hooligan, the enlisted man, the partying bartender, the drug dealer, the addict, the man on the journey to sobriety, the businessman, the veteran, the family man, the man of faith. To look at one side of Patrick does not capture his story. You must take every angle and piece them together into the rich tapestry of his life to begin understanding who he is and what motivates him.

For three years, I wrestled with the pieces of Patrick, trying to create a picture of the man I had come to know. I restarted this book three times, trying to find the right words. But then, in a flash, I understood that the pieces were not the whole picture. In between the pieces were seemingly blank spaces. It was in studying those spaces that I truly saw Patrick. Because in the empty spaces were the threads of God's grace, protection, and forgiveness that stitched everything together and created the man.

Through his story, I understand that God takes every part of who we are, even the unseemly ones, and creates a beautiful masterpiece. Patrick's life is a beacon of hope in the darkest times because there is nothing that you cannot overcome and change with determination, commitment, and God's grace.

REFERENCES

The Burning of Will Shuster's Zozobra. (2021, November 9). Retrieved February 8, 2022, from https://burnzozobra.com/all-about-zozobra/

CIA-Contra-crack cocaine controversy. (n.d.). Retrieved February 8, 2022, from https://oig.justice.gov/sites/default/files/archive/special/9712/ch01p1.htm

Dictionary.com. (n.d.). *Pin boy definition & meaning.* Dictionary.com. Retrieved February 8, 2022, from https://www.dictionary.com/browse/pin-boy

Downrange warriors. Downrange Warriors. (n.d.). Retrieved February 8, 2022, from https://www.downrangewarriors.org/

Glass history. Indiana Glass Trail. (n.d.). Retrieved February 8, 2022, from https://indianaglasstrail.com/glass-history/#:~:text=On%20October%206%2C%201886%2C%20a,a%20depth%20of%20900%20feet.&text=Firms%20such%20as%20the%20Indiana,of%20pressed%20and%20blown%20decorative

Gleason, D. (2018, January 3). *The legend of the lost dutchman Mine - C&I Magazine.* Cowboys and Indians Magazine. Retrieved February 8,

2022, from https://www.cowboysindians.com/2018/01/the-legend-of-the-lost-dutchman-mine/#:~:text=In%202009%2C%20Denver%20bellhop%20Jesse,of%20a%2018Ofoot%2Dfoot%20cliff

Has the location of Noah's ark finally been proven using 3D scans? The Jerusalem Post | JPost.com. (n.d.). Retrieved February 8, 2022, from https://www.jpost.com/archaeology/has-the-location-of-noahs-ark-finally-been-proven-using-3d-scans-680890

History.com Editors. (2017, July 13). *Knights Templar.* History.com. Retrieved February 8, 2022, from https://www.history.com/topics/middle-ages/the-knights-templar

In memory honor roll. Vietnam Veterans Memorial Fund. (2020, January 27). Retrieved February 8, 2022, from https://www.vvmf.org/Honor-Roll/500834/James-Edwin-Richcreek-Sr/

Joshua Jarvis (1848-1918) - find a grave memorial. Find a Grave. (n.d.). Retrieved February 8, 2022, from https://www.findagrave.com/memorial/38377520/joshua-jarvis

Matter park. WikiMarion. (n.d.). Retrieved February 8, 2022, from http://www.wikimarion.org/Matter_Park

Muncie history. Discover Muncie. (2021, January 15). Retrieved February 8, 2022, from https://discovermuncie.com/history-of-muncie/

The problem. Sound Off. (n.d.). Retrieved February 8, 2022, from
https://sound-off.com/the-
problem/?gclid=CjwKCAiAo4OQBhBBEiwA5KWu_-
GFiPFXGuRP353GPJY8fweunnFj15qR95WAvvRrSzciF5m89cbBox
oCcoUQAvD_BwE

Racial Incident Police Report, July 4, 1967. Indiana Memory. (n.d.).
Retrieved February 8, 2022, from
https://digital.library.in.gov/Record/SJCPL_p16827coll4-2760

Rozen-Wheeler, contributed by: A. (2020, January 5). *Marion,
Indiana lynching (1930)* •. •. Retrieved February 8, 2022, from
https://www.blackpast.org/african-american-history/marion-indiana-
lynching-1930/

Schooneveld, I. van. (2020, August 4). *Lifelong spiritual bond between
the Kazakh Eagle Hunter and his Golden Bird.* Sinchi Foundation.
Retrieved February 8, 2022, from https://sinchi-
foundation.com/news/kazakh-eagle-hunter-and-his-golden-
bird/#:~:text=Training%20continues%20by%20dragging%20a,return
%20after%20killing%20their%20prey.

St Vincent Villa. Facebook. (n.d.). Retrieved February 8, 2022,
from https://www.facebook.com/pages/category/Religious-
Organization/Saint-Vincent-Villa-Catholic-Orphanage-of-Fort-
Wayne-Indiana-361227217528

St. Vincent Villa, Fort Wayne, Indiana. Indiana Memory. (n.d.). Retrieved February 8, 2022, from https://digital.library.in.gov/Record/ACPL_GenealogyCenter-581

Superstition Mountain Museum (apache junction) - 2022 all you need to know before you go (with photos). Tripadvisor. (n.d.). Retrieved February 8, 2022, from https://www.tripadvisor.com/Attraction_Review-g29033-d2624665-Reviews-Superstition_Mountain_Museum-Apache_Junction_Arizona.htm

Thomas, C. (2021, February 22). *On horseback among the eagle hunters and herders of the Mongolian altai.* The New York Times. Retrieved February 8, 2022, from https://www.nytimes.com/2021/02/22/travel/mongolia-eagle-hunters.html#:~:text=surround%20Tolbo%20Lake.-,Deep%20in%20the%20Altai%20Mountains%2C%20where%20Russia%2C%20China%2C%20Kazakhstan,foxes%20and%20other%20small%20animals.

US Department of Commerce, N. O. A. A. (2021, November 5). *April 11th 1965 Palm Sunday tornado outbreak.* National Weather Service. Retrieved February 8, 2022, from https://www.weather.gov/iwx/1965_palmsunday_50

Weather history for Marion, Grant County, in. Almanac.com. (n.d.). Retrieved February 8, 2022, from https://www.almanac.com/weather/history/IN/Marion%2C%20Grant%20County/1968-11-15

Wikimedia Foundation. (2021, October 21). *Sossusvlei*. Wikipedia. Retrieved February 8, 2022, from https://en.wikipedia.org/wiki/Sossusvlei

Wikimedia Foundation. (2022, February 4). *Sonny Barger*. Wikipedia. Retrieved February 8, 2022, from https://en.wikipedia.org/wiki/Sonny_Barger

Wikimedia Foundation. (2022, February 4). *St. Vincent villa historic district*. Wikipedia. Retrieved February 8, 2022, from https://en.wikipedia.org/wiki/St._Vincent_Villa_Historic_District

Wikimedia Foundation. (2022, January 18). *1965 Palm Sunday tornado outbreak*. Wikipedia. Retrieved February 8, 2022, from https://en.wikipedia.org/wiki/1965_Palm_Sunday_tornado_outbreak

Wikimedia Foundation. (2022, January 22). *Iran–Contra affair*. Wikipedia. Retrieved February 8, 2022, from https://en.wikipedia.org/wiki/Iran%E2%80%93Contra_affair

Printed in Great Britain
by Amazon

39165856R00116